Raku, Pit & Barrel

Firing
Techniques

Raku, Pit & Barrel

Ceramic
Arts
Handbook
Series

Edited by Anderson Turner

The American Ceramic Society
600 N. Cleveland Ave., Suite 210
Westerville, Ohio 43082

www.CeramicArtsDaily.org

The American Ceramic Society
600 N. Cleveland Ave., Suite 210
Westerville, OH 43082

11 10 09 08   5 4 3 2

ISBN: 978-1-57498-288-6

Publisher: Charles Spahr, President, Ceramic Publications Company, a wholly owned subsidiary of The American Ceramic Society

Art Book Program Manager: Bill Jones

Series Editor: Anderson Turner

Graphic Design and Production: Melissa Bury, Bury Design, Westerville, Ohio

Cover Images: Bottles by Frank James Fisher, Vessel by Martha Puckett and "Blue and Red Raku Box on Ball Feet" by Tim Proud

Frontispiece: "Globe Pot" by Jimmy Clark

Photo credits: All photos by authors or artists except for the following: Lee Fatherree and Rossen Townsend (1-5); Jay Bechemin (40-46); Paul Breadner (56-60); Ron Bolander (73-76); S.B. Khalsa (77); Mike Keller and Dan Woodrum (81-84); Randy Batista (89-91); Ed Abrahamson, Jonas Grushkin, and Clint Swink (93-99); Kelpie, Heini Schneebeli (113-116).

Printed in China

Contents

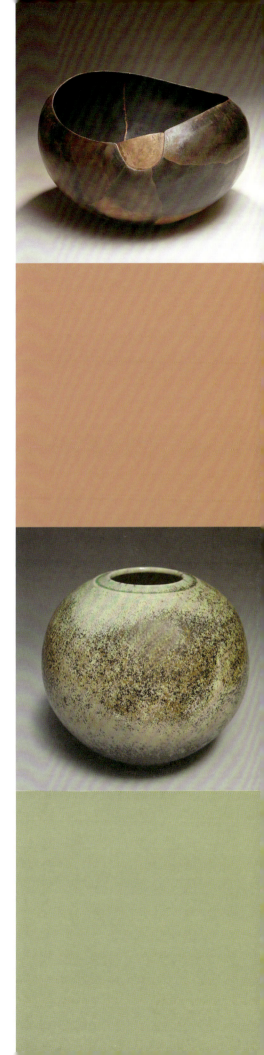

Preface

My earliest art memory is making beads and small pots out of clay with my mother, sister and several of my mother's friends. We wrapped each piece in newspaper and buried them in a metal trashcan with sawdust and larger scraps of wood. I think Mom actually dug a pit in the ground to put the can in, though I'm not sure why she felt this was necessary. I remember they had some difficulty keeping the thing burning. However, with a handy drill and an awl, airflow was established and the pieces started their long can-in-a-pit firing. I think we still have some of the beads from this firing on some of the jewelry my daughters use for dress up. I always know the pieces because of their blackness and their ultra 1970s four-year-old kid's handmade aesthetic.

Mom and I reproduced this process a few times throughout the years. We would buy a small metal can that would fit in our fireplace and then either buy clay and make things, or purchase greenware of some kind, find some sawdust, then fire away. It's really a straightforward process and some of our best gifts for friends and loved ones came out of these little firings.

As I've read through these articles I've often thought of that first pit experience. It's made me realize how lucky I am to have the family I have; also it's been a great re-energizer. There's just something about fire that I think every person who loves clay relates to because it speaks to the soul and excites the mind. In undergraduate school I did room-sized installation pieces out of little clay parts that I elected to raku. I can't believe my professor put up with that!

Regardless of whether or not you've had similar experiences in your history, raku, pit and barrel firing are exciting ways to fire and create interesting surfaces on your work. Not only are the processes romantic ones that allude to a different place and time, but they're also variable, with results that often occur with a degree of chance. Even the most skilled professional can only control what the results *should* be like, not exactly what they *will* be like. Because of this fact I believe that these processes are also some of our best educational tools. I know several beginning throwing or handbuilding classes that require students to only raku their pieces. However, whether you're a beginner or an established ceramic artist, I know you'll find something in these pages to inspire and energize you.

Anderson Turner

Hal Riegger
Raku Pioneer

by Gregg Allen Lindsley

It is rare indeed when a lifetime of work in any discipline is assembled for viewing. It is even more rare to be able to view a body of work that reflects nearly all the works produced in that discipline around the world today. Such an event took place November 27–December 30, 2004, at TRAX Gallery in Berkeley, California, when raku pioneer Hal Riegger was honored with a retrospective show featuring a lifetime of work.

Riegger, a gentle giant of a man, brought a rigorous discipline to the study of raku, a study that, for him, began in the spring of 1952. He discovered an account of Japanese raku practices by Warren Gilbertson in an old (February 1943) issue of the *The Bulletin of the American Ceramic Society*. After reading about the technique, Riegger built a small kiln and began firing. His first attempts met with limited success, but he became increasingly involved and, in 1958, taught raku for the first time at Haystack Mountain School of Crafts in Deer Isle, Maine.

To say his was an ordinary life of clay and academia would be to grossly misstate the facts and underestimate the man. After earning his bachelors degree at Alfred University and completing his resident work on his masters degree at The Ohio State University in 1939, his pottery life was both interrupted and enhanced by World War II. Riegger was a conscientious objector, morally opposed to war, a stance he attributes to the education he received at the School of Organic Education in Fairhope, Alabama, where students were allowed to pursue their own interests in their own time, which allowed their deepest interests and abilities to come naturally to the surface. World War II conscientious objectors were organized into work camps and were required to pay to stay there. Riegger was assigned to a camp in northwestern North Dakota, where he helped organize a pottery program for the men in the camp. The program gained national attention for the quality of the work produced, and an exhibition of assignees' work toured veteran's hospitals to encourage physical therapy.

Bowl, 16 inches in diameter, wheel-thrown stoneware, with glaze, and trailed and brushed slip decoration, 1947.

Riegger's work over the years has influenced everyone who has worked making raku. It is a tribute to his rather shy and unassuming nature that he felt he really hasn't influenced anyone. Others disagree. Former student, Yolanda Samuels, remembers how taking classes from Riegger at the California College of Arts and Crafts in 1956 changed her entire outlook on clay. "I started my clay career working with Marguerite Wildenhain, and her approach was

very strict. Hal, on the other hand, had us experimenting with everything. He was so open, it was like I could finally be really creative."

Berkeley potter and TRAX gallery collaborator Robert Brady remembers his first meeting with Riegger. "I was very impressed with Hal, his work, house and lifestyle. Hal lived very simply, somewhere between a Zen Bhuddist and Shaker sensibility. He did not surround himself with more than he needed. His wardrobe was very simple; khaki shorts, white tee shirts and work shoes. His pots were much the same—beautiful, simple volumes, economically made. They were very light and struck a chord with my own sensibilities."

A traditionalist when it comes to raku, Riegger's study of the Japanese tea ceremony, the purpose of the teabowls and the method of their making, helped him to realize that he had a deep affinity for Japanese culture and an innate understanding of what was behind the making of ceremonial ware.

His exposure to, and assimilation of, Japanese raku led him to believe that the creation of raku without an underlining understanding of why a piece is made lacks the human intent which makes work come alive. This is an attitude that was reinforced by his days in the camp.

For Riegger, raku refered to those pieces made specifically for the tea ceremony, and executed with the precepts appropriate to things of fired clay made for the ceremony. All other work is not raku, but done in the raku style. "I don't like much of what is being made in the name of raku today. It's too loud; it hits you in the face. Raku pots should be quiet. You should have to search them out," he said. "In fact, I don't think a person with a big ego could make a raku pot.

"People come to see me make raku," Riegger said. "There really isn't much to see. You pull the pieces out of the kiln, put it in sawdust, cover it with a can, and walk away.

Teabowl, 3½ inches in height, red clay, raku fired, 2000.

Then you come back later and there is the pot. People are so disappointed. They think there should be some kind of party going on!

"In American ceramics history," said Riegger, "raku followed stoneware, and became an alternative to stoneware's earthy color palette because bright, lustrous colors could be obtained. The exciting finishes obtained have led to people grabbing any old pot and putting glaze on it with no thought to how the glaze fits the pot."

Riegger noted that post-firing reduction was not part of Japanese raku. So where did the reduction come from? Herbert H. Sanders, in his *World of Japanese Ceramics*, explains that, when the clay was bisqued in a wood or charcoal kiln,

Plate, 9 inches in length, with brushed and trailed glaze

the clay was reduced in certain areas. These spots of reduction remained in the clay, under the glaze, when they were glaze fired. These pots were highly sought after and greatly prized.

Riegger's asymmetrical shapes show a quality of freedom and abandonment. Pots made this way show a quality that is human. He believed that smaller is more powerful. For instance, a black glaze applied to a pot with just a spot of luster makes for a strong and beautiful piece, as opposed to a loud, brightly colored piece.

Hal Riegger: Teacher and Friend

by Steven Branfman

I first saw raku in 1974 as a graduate student at Rhode Island School of Design (RISD). My introduction was less than elegant. In fact, it was crude. A few students were huddled around a small kiln with the door half open. They were reaching in with long-handled tongs and removing pots in a most haphazard, random fashion. One of them asked, "are they ready?" Another replied, "I have no idea." Within their dubiousness was an excitement and spontaneity that attracted me. Alas, RISD was focused on high firing. If I wanted to pursue raku, I was on my own. To the library I went and there I found *Raku: Art and Technique* by Hal Riegger. That night I read it cover to cover. The highlighted passages and notes left in the margins by previous readers spoke volumes to the book's importance and influence. The next day I bought a copy of my own. That book became my bible and Riegger became my teacher.

Riegger taught me about the origins of raku, its intent and the philosophy that surrounds it. He taught me about clay, glazes and kilns. I learned the difference between crude and primitive. He had a profound influence on my work and my eventual decision to pursue raku exclusively.

Fast forward to 1989 when I was writing a book on raku. Where better to begin than with the person whose book started my career. Finding Riegger wasn't difficult, despite the fact that his name and identity had all but vanished from the clay scene. I telephoned him, and there began a friendship that I wish had begun sooner. We spoke by phone, then by letters as his hearing began to fail, and then, one day, I received an e-mail. This 80-something was not one to sit idly by as technology whizzed past. At first we talked about clay and pots and, of course, raku. Soon, conversation included experience, family, friends, accomplishments, delights and disappointments. We exchanged gifts and artifacts. I learned of the people with whom he'd crossed paths and soon realized how important an individual he was (not through his boasting or even suggestion). He criticized me and I questioned him. I took it as a badge of honor when I learned that at a workshop he used a small vessel I had given him as an example of a misguided application of raku. As the years went by, our friendship grew, our bond became stronger, and our respect for each other greater. Our conversations became focused on purpose, life and legacy.

A new raku facility was built at his alma mater, The New York State College of Ceramics at Alfred University in New York, and named in his honor. A presidential citation and plaque recognize his lifetime devoted to clay and celebrate his formidable contributions to the history of American ceramics. I was proud to accept it on my friend's behalf. His quiet, humble approach to his work and life are the very personal qualities that delayed this honor for so long.

Plate, 9 inches in length, white clay, with brushed and trailed red slip, raku fired, 2002.

Karen Shapiro
The Art of Everyday Life

by Lisa Crawford Watson

"Half & Half,"
16½ inches
in height, cone 10
white stoneware,
bisque fired to
cone 04, brushed
and sprayed
with commercial
underglazes,
fired to cone 06,
then glazed
and raku fired.

Art imitates life—particularly for those who recognize it in the common elements of their everyday surroundings. There is the sculptural curve of a coffeepot, the etching on a bar of soap, the texture of an orange. The creative eye can see it; the creative hand will render it.

Karen Shapiro derives her art from everyday life. Her ceramic sculpture doesn't have to be studied, interpreted or understood. It is what it is.

"Throughout my youth," Shapiro recalled, "I was always striving for the perfect art form. When I tried to do it as a grown-up, it didn't come so easily. Mid-struggle, I looked over at my coffeepot and milk carton and thought, 'Wow!' When you get older, you realize everything is right there."

Shapiro's sculptures represent items that have been used, and they look it. Whether it's a box of Morton salt or a heroic tube of Great Lash mascara, each piece speaks to an era or a season, an event or a time, when it was a part of the life of the viewer.

"I call them pop icons, except they have a little surface development, a patina, that gives them a friendly, used quality," observes Chris Winfield. "Some pieces, many of which are from packaging of the 1930s, '40s and '50s, are quite nostalgic. They have a historical element but are still around, which gives them their popular appeal. Collectors tend to put them on a kitchen counter or vanity, places where the actual items would go."

Virginia Breier, describes the work as "technically incredible and very

After the initial bisque firing, Shapiro applies surface detail by brushing or spraying underglazes over graphic tape, contact paper cutouts, latex and other resist materials, then fires to cone 06. The final step for each piece is the firing of a crackle glaze and postfiring reduction.

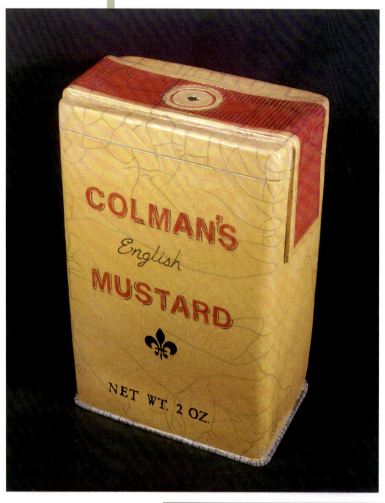

"Colman's Mustard," 12 inches in height, cone 10 white stoneware, bisque fired to cone 04, brushed and sprayed with underglazes, refired to cone 06, then glazed and raku fired.

appealing because of their humor. So often, when something is large, it gives you a different perspective on how you would look at the object so common to you. It makes us laugh. Karen is a very clever woman."

Don Endemann, who met Shapiro through Breier and later introduced her to Winfield, considers her work "comfort clay" with much the same appeal as comfort food. "Everybody smiles when they look at her work," said Endemann. "It fills a nostalgia, spanning generations of folks who have handled the original forms. What I like about her work is that it's very straightforward. She makes each piece individual and unique."

Although Shapiro considers herself a new kid in the ceramics circle, the techniques of kneading, forming, carving and glazing are not new to her. For 30 years, she worked as a pastry chef, sculpting the ultimate edible art form.

Her career developed without a plan, without expectations—except to be creative. A design major in college, she was vacillating between careers in fashion or package design, when she decided to marry and support someone else's career. "Then,"

"It Never Rains," 13 inches in height, cone 10 white stoneware, bisque fired to cone 04, brushed and sprayed with commercial underglazes, fired to cone 06, then glazed and raku fired.

Shapiro says, "it was my turn. I was looking around for what area of art I wanted to pursue, and started cooking as a hobby. And there it went. I loved it for 20 of my 30 years as a pastry chef. In making a move to ceramics, I realized I had all the tools to roll out dough. I just used them to roll out clay. All my marzipan tools went to clay."

When Shapiro took a ceramics class with Anne Peete Carrington at the College of Marin, she realized, "I love clay; I should get back to this. It was Anne who said, 'You're on your way to becoming an artist.' She gave me the confidence and the basic techniques I needed to succeed in this new medium."

Pastry chefs, as a rule, are a detail-oriented group. For Shapiro, the most engaging aspect of decorating cakes had been the precision artistry, the graphic and sculptural elements. It still is, and it shows in her ceramics.

Just as she sees the artistry in mundane objects, she frequently encounters the tools of her trade in ordinary items, as well. "There isn't something on the market designed specifically for doing graphics on clay," she said, "but I went out and found what would work. I use adhesive paper or vinyl lettering to make a stencil. I use airbrushing and various things to create my finishes. For instance, when I wanted something to look like dirt, I used dirt; it worked. It's always challenging to find what I need to mash into the clay or cut it out, but I come up with it."

"Goldfish" and "Milanos," 21 inches in height, white stoneware, bisque fired to cone 04, brushed and sprayed with commercial underglazes, fired to cone 06, then glazed and raku fired.

"Great Lash," 21 inches in height, handbuilt white stoneware, with underglazes and glaze, raku fired, by Karen Shapiro, Gualala, California.

She enjoys the process of rolling out, cutting and forming her slab-built pieces, but it's the glazing and firing that take the cake. "I use a high-fire clay, which I low fire because I raku," Shapiro said of the technique she learned from Carrington. "My pieces are initially electric fired, frequently a second time with the underglazes and graphics on them.

"If I'm doing some kind of modern piece of everyday life, and I kind of funk it up with raku, I can get wonderful flecks and cracks that age it, bring it to life. If I stopped with the electric firing, it would look like the item, but more like a toy. The raku firing [in a gas kiln in her backyard] puts in the wonderful imperfections of real life.

"I bring the temperature up to cone 08, which is orange-red, then immediately open the kiln, reach in with tongs, remove the piece and put it in a trash can. The excitement of reaching into a red-hot environment, of the flaming can—even the choking smoke—of finding results I never dreamed of has given me enormous energy, appetite and passion for my work."

Dazzling Crackles

by Sumi von Dassow

**Vessel,
6 inches high,
by Jim Chamberlain.
B-Mix clay with clear
crackle glaze.**

If you put a white glaze on a raku pot, fire it until the glaze melts then put it in your reduction barrel, the glaze will crackle. While crackle glazes aren't as finicky as copper luster glazes, there are things you can do to maximize the amount of crackling you'll get for a truly striking effect.

Jim Chamberlain, a fire fighter and a potter, has made something of a specialty of perfecting the white crackle glaze. His big secret? Compressed air. Once the glaze has melted, instead of putting the pot directly into the reduction barrel, he sprays it with canned compressed air to cause the glaze surface to quickly cool and contract, thus encouraging the formation of bold, distinct glaze cracks.

Raku pots usually develop a network of fine cracks overall, more or less automatically, simply from exposure to the cool air when the kiln is opened. Much trickier, you would think, to avoid a crackle pattern than to encourage it! For those wanting to help the process along, standard practice is often to wait a couple of minutes or to wave the pot in the air a few times before putting the pot into the barrel. This method gives the pot time to develop an extensive crackle network, however, when using compressed air, the glaze often ends up with a secondary network of bold black lines.

Although this technique really is as simple as it sounds, there is one caveat to keep in mind. The rapid and forced cooling of the pot upon removal from the kiln is relatively hard on the structure of the pot itself. An excessively thin, thick or uneven pot is likely to crack under the strain. Also, a wide platter is less likely to survive the treatment than a narrow-mouthed jar or vase. Although it's possible to use a variety of clays, from standard raku clays to smooth white stoneware clay, the groggier raku clay is more likely to withstand the temperature differential. You have to be prepared to accept a certain amount of loss when experimenting with this technique!

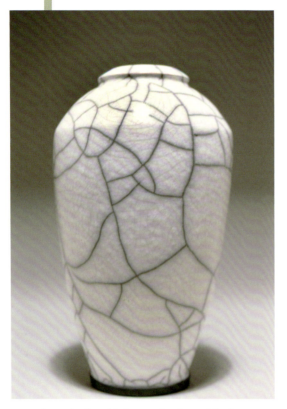

Vessel, 7½ inches high, B-Mix clay with clear crackle glaze.

Jim uses the clear crackle raku glaze recipe. He masks off areas he wants unglazed and applies this glaze by spraying. The recipe came from Gary Ferguson of Caldwell, Idaho.

Vessel, 8 inches high, speckled buff clay with clear crackle glaze.

Recipe

Ferguson's White Crackle

Gerstley Borate	65 %
Nepheline Syenite	20
EPK Kaolin	5
Silica Flint	10
	100 %

Vessel, 8 inches high, B-Mix clay with clear crackle glaze, by Jim Chamberlain.

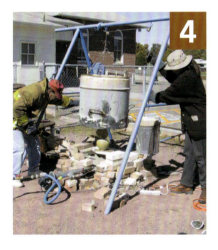

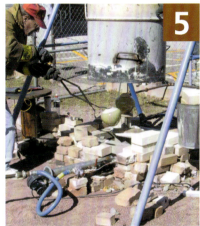

The raku setup features a cut-down oil drum lined with fiber, and a pail of bricks supported on an old swing-set frame as a counterweight to open the kiln (figure 1). There are two burners for quick and even heating, and Jim monitors the temperature with a pyrometer.

The kiln is loaded with pots that have been preheated in an electric kiln to prevent cracking from thermal shock (figure 2). Jim often places pots on pieces of shelf raised with shelf supports to get them into the hottest part of the kiln. Usually, only two pieces are fired at a time.

Although the kiln can reach final temperature in 20 minutes, Jim prefers to raise the temperature a little more slowly, allowing the pots 30 minutes to reach their final temperature of about 1860°F (figure 3).

The gas is shut off and the kiln is opened (figure 4). This kiln is easier to open with an assistant to load the counterweight bucket with bricks and guide it down.

With the kiln open Jim quickly removes the pots with tongs (figure 5). A professional fire fighter, Jim wears his work coat and leather gloves for protection.

Jim removes the pots from the kiln and places them on preheated bricks (figure 6). He leaves them on the bricks for a few seconds until he hears the glaze beginning to "ping" as it shrinks and crackles.

The pots are sprayed on all sides with canned compressed air (figure 10). Jim finds it easier to use the cans than dragging an air-compressor out to the raku yard. Although this is more expensive, one can will spray quite a few pots. He notes that it is also possible to use a small fan, although the air from a fan can't be aimed so precisely.

Jim places still-hot pots into the newspaper-lined reduction barrels (figure 11). Although the pots are hot enough to light the newspaper, by this time the glaze has set enough that the pot's surface isn't

damaged when it touches the reduction materials.

To assure lots of smoke, and to help insulate the pot while it cools slowly, Jim quickly covers the pots with plenty of wood shavings (figure 12). If the pot has escaped cracking by this point, its chances of survival are pretty good.

Once the shavings have started smoking, the barrels are covered and left to smoke for at least an hour (figure 13). The entire process of opening the kiln to covering the barrels has taken barely three minutes.

What's a Raku Glaze?

by Steven Branfman

In my workshops, I get asked many questions but never "What is a raku glaze?" Why? Because everyone knows what a raku glaze is. Right? It's a glaze that is labeled "raku." Wrong. It's time to expand your thinking and understand exactly what this whole raku glaze thing is about.

A raku glaze is any glaze you use in the raku method. It doesn't have to be a glaze specifically designed for raku, formulated to fire at the temperature you fire your raku to, nor homemade or commercial. It can be most anything. The key to success is understanding the raku firing process and the ability to predict how a particular glaze reacts to that process.

Raku as practiced in the West is a low-fire method in which we quickly heat the ware, remove the ware from the kiln when the glaze has melted, and perform some type of post-firing process to the piece. The post-firing phase is usually an immersion in an organic combustible material to affect the final outcome on the glaze and the raw clay. Deciding when the glaze has melted takes practice and is best done by observation, though many potters use pyrometers to aid in making that decision. Raku is exciting, often unpredictable to the novice and fun to do.

Glaze Application

Glazing work for raku can be done by all the methods known—dipping, pouring, brushing, spraying, splashing, dripping, sponging—you name it. Glazes also can be used alone or in combination. Keep in mind that the application of a glaze has a direct effect on the result.

Dedicated Raku Glazes

Glazes specifically designed for raku fall into two categories—homemade and commercially prepared. If you mix your own, you'll find scores of recipes. Search the internet, ask friends, look in any book on glazes or raku and look in magazines. In no time you will find more glazes than you could use in a lifetime. Of course, to mix your own glazes you must have a stock of materials, mix-

Sprayed stoneware glaze under clear raku glaze, by Steven Branfman.

Brushed stoneware glaze under clear raku glaze.

ing paraphernalia, knowledge and interest. If this doesn't turn you on there are myriad manufacturers that produce almost as many raku glazes. The advantage of using commercial glazes is that you are given instruction on how to use the glaze, you have a sample of the fired glaze to help guide your results, and the formulation (although not the results!) will be consistent time after time. Of course, commercial glazes are a bit more expensive than mixing your own, and by using commercial glazes you are removing what is for some, the most interesting part of the raku process: designing and using your own glazes.

Low-Fire Glazes

Glazes used in the raku process need not be "raku" glazes at all. At its core, raku is a low-temperature firing method. The fact that we remove the ware from the kiln while the pots are hot and the glaze is molten is irrelevant. Understanding this opens up a whole new world of glazes. Any glaze that is formulated to fire at the low temperature of raku can be used. First, you must decide at what temperature you are firing. Most raku is done in the cone 010–06 range. Begin by choosing glazes that both appeal to you in color and that fire in your range. You will have to experiment but I have never found a glaze that I couldn't use successfully.

High-Fire Glazes

We are not limited only to glazes that melt at the low temperatures. With greater understanding of the raku process, even mid-range and high-fire glazes can be used in the low-temperature range of raku. Try using your regular stoneware glazes as slips. Over the glaze, apply a clear or white raku or other low-temperature glaze. The low-temperature glaze causes the high-fire glaze to melt giving you a new palette of colors to work with.

Other Glazes

In addition to glazes, slips, engobes, underglazes, overglazes, china paints, underglaze pencils, oxides and stains are all viable in the raku process.

Food Safety

No matter what type of glaze or decorative material you use, raku is inherently unsafe for use as domestic ware. The rapid firing, removal of the ware and subsequent post-firing phase all contribute to fragility, porosity, and thin, easily flaked glaze surfaces. Not all materials used in raku glazes are toxic. In fact, most are not. Confusion arises when you realize that over the centuries some of the most prized teabowls by tea masters have been raku fired. Be safe, and think of your raku ware as decorative and not functional.

Multilayered brushed commercial low-fire glazes.

Raku Glazing
An Alternative Look

by Steven Branfman

Vessel, 15 inches in height, combed and incised surface, brushed and splattered commercial low-fire glaze, raku fired, by Steven Branfman.

Raku—even those new to clay and the various ways in which it can be fired have some notion and make some assumptions about raku. Most often, the image that is conjured up is a roaring, flaming kiln, an unusual collection of tools more commonly seen next to a fireplace or welding station, metal cans and enough smoke to summon the regional fire department. What's also most commonly envisioned is the expected result of high copper luster, white crackle glaze and black, raw surfaces. Of course, this is not surprising as the lure of copper, bronze and pearl-like iridescence contrasted with the black or gray of an unglazed area is attractive, can be startling and is often seen as exotic.

For good or for bad, raku is a technique that's simple in concept, requires rudimentary firing facilities and is easy to do. Because of this simplicity, many wares display superficial aesthetics and lack individuality and power. The kind of effects described above offer an exhilarating and sometimes intoxicating foray into the technique, but the excitement that they stir can be short lived, not to mention commonplace. A deeper understanding of the process along with experimentation and higher expectations can yield sophisticated colors, textures and surfaces not necessarily recognized as "raku."

The Western Raku Method

Raku as we practice it in the West is a low-fire method in which we quickly heat the ware, remove it from the kiln when the glaze has melted, and perform some type of post-firing process to the piece. Though the post-firing phase is not part of the traditional Japanese practice, it has become the signature of Western raku. The post-firing phase is usually an immersion in sawdust or some other organic combustible material in order to affect the final outcome on the glaze and the raw clay.

Process

Every step of my process is predicted and planned. My choice of glazes and application of those glazes determines the firing. Though some potters use pyrometers or even cones in their raku firings to carefully judge glaze maturity, I find that doing this eliminates an important degree of variability and control. The most important component of my firing is the degree to which I allow the glazes to melt and flow. Since I'm using glazes that mature at different temperatures, careful observation of the surface is necessary to achieve the "correct" melting. My intention is to have some areas smooth and glossy, some not quite as melted, and others with the appearance of dry and underfired glaze. I can also control the degree to which poured glaze runs and drips over the surface of the pot by how much I allow it to melt.

Deciding when the glaze has melted takes practice and is best done by visual observation, though many potters use pyrometers to aid in making that decision.

There are many aspects to the raku technique, all of which have the potential to affect the final outcome, and all of which require practice, experimentation, trial and error and patience. Here, we'll concentrate on so-called "alternative" glazes; that is, glazes not usually associated with, or understood to be used in the raku technique. I will also discuss methods of application that have the

potential to yield new and exciting surfaces and results.

Getting Started

Though there's no accepted standard firing temperature for raku, most potters fire between cone 010 and 06. I have a collection of commercial low-fire glazes and underglazes, all of which are perfectly suitable for raku firing (figure 1). In addition to low-fire glazes and underglazes, I also routinely use cone 6 and cone 10 stoneware glazes (figure 2). There will be more on their use later. I also use homemade low-fire and so-

called "raku" glazes. The brushes I use are inexpensive Chinese bristle brushes designed to be used and thrown away. Throw away? No way! These are my favorite brushes and they're available in any paint or home center.

My glazing method centers around applying thin, multiple layers of glaze (figure 3). While the application appears to be quite random, it's carefully planned and executed. I may use a single glaze or as many as fifteen different glazes on a single piece. The brushes I use are perfectly suited as they do not hold much glaze and they transfer glaze very unevenly. I draw the brush lightly over the surface of the pot, depositing varying thicknesses of glaze (figure 4).

With each successive layer, the surface gets deeper and the glaze coating becomes more and more variable. Most of my pots have deep-ly textured surfaces to begin with. My application is intended to accentuate the texture in the clay. In certain areas the thickness and unevenness of glaze becomes a texture in and of itself.

Other methods of application that I use frequently are splattering (figure 5), dripping and very controlled pouring (figure 6). These approaches add movement and contrast to the somewhat static effect achieved by the way I brush. Experimenting with the thickness of glaze for pouring will give you different results depending on the way the glaze runs, drips and melts.

Though we all know to thoroughly mix a glaze before using it, there are times when I either don't bother or I will purposely gather glaze from the inside wall or lid of the bucket or jar (figure 7). Doing this often gives you an "incomplete" glaze that may offer unusual and unpredictable results.

Firing Process

My firing site contains six kilns of different sizes and types, including four recycled electric kilns fired with propane, a wood-fired kiln and kiln manufactured by Ceramic Services of Chino, California (figure 8). The site is clean, organized and has plenty of space. Successful firing requires planning, choreography and concentration, which results in a calm atmosphere. I always fire with the help of a single assistant.

After carefully examining the surfaces for desirable glaze melt, a piece is removed from the kiln (figure 9). Bowls and small pieces are taken with tongs directly through the flue hole in the top of the kiln.

An assistant removes the lid so I can retrieve a larger piece with tongs (figure 10).

Next, he sprays areas of the surface with water (figure 11). This brightens the glazes and reduces the likelihood of copper lusters. You can also control cooling by pouring water onto your piece as you would pour a glaze, or by using compressed air.

After sufficient spraying, the piece is placed in a small metal container, sprinkled with coarse sawdust, allowed to flame, then covered (figure 12).

Being patient and allowing the piece to cool to the touch before opening the container all but eliminates cracking due to fast cooling (figure 13).

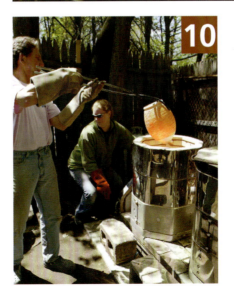

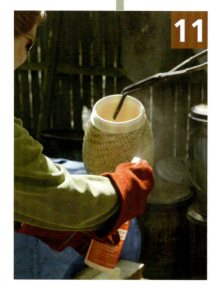

Glazes

Glazes are always formulated and designed to be fired within certain cone ranges. However, when using glazes for strictly decorative purposes, the prescribed firing range can be ignored. Raku, with its style of visual observation to determine glaze readiness, lends itself perfectly to experimenting with glazes that mature at different temperatures. If used alone, high-fire glazes will be very dry and slip-like at the low temperatures of raku. If combined with low-fire or raku glazes, contact with these glazes will flux the high-fire glazes causing them to melt (more or less). I have a random stock of commercial low-fire glazes and underglazes that I have collected over the years. Use what you have, what you can find and what is available.

Raku ware must be cleaned to rid the piece of soot, ash and carbon that gets deposited on the surface (figure 14). Use an abrasive cleaner and scrub brush or steel wool. Anything that washes off is supposed to come off!

Recipes

Basic White Crackle

Gerstley Borate	65 %
Tin Oxide	12
Nepheline Syenite	15
Tenn Ball Clay	5
Silica	5
	100 %

An opaque white glaze.

Rogers White

Spodumene	35 %
Gerstley Borate	60
Tennessee Ball Clay	5
	100 %

Though it is called "white," this is actually a transparent glaze.

Kelley's Low-Fire Shino

Lithium Carbonate	26 %
Nepheline Syenite	64
EPK Kaolin	10
	100 %
Add: Light Rutile	6.0%
Manganese Carbonate	0.5%

This is a semi-opaque glaze with excellent crackle and lovely tan to silvery color characteristics and texture depending on firing temp. Works well in combination with other glazes.

Teabowl, 3 inches in height, carved and altered, with Kelly's Low-Fire Shino, raku fired, by Steven Branfman.

Raku is a technique loaded with creative possibilities. A kaleidoscope of colors and surface effects can be achieved. Learn and become comfortable with the basic process by reading, and taking a class or workshop. Then, expand your practice with your own individuality, personality and character.

Peel-Away Slip in a Hurry

by Mark S. Richardson

Jar, 7 inches in height, porcelain raku fixed with peel-away slip, by Mark Richardson.

After accepting a commission for 90 small covered jars, with crackled smoke decoration, I began to research all that was written about using and firing peel-away slip. I had used it before in my classes, but I had never worked out all the details that were required to complete 90 objects efficiently and successfully. After throwing 120 jars and lids, I felt I had enough to begin the challenge of firing. I used a raku kiln and had some difficulty at first getting the slip to stay on through the firing. Even if it did make it through the kiln, I had trouble getting the jars into the reduction barrel without disturbing the slip. After a few failures, I came up with a system that was easy to use and produced great results.

Before starting to fire the jars, I made a basket with handles to fit inside the kiln. I used a food grate from a grill as a base and then made a cylinder around the grate with heavy-duty hardware cloth (a metal netting available at most large lumberyards or hardware stores). The sections were bound together with

#10 binding wire and the handle was made by winding the binding wire repeatedly around the top of the cylinder. I made the loops large enough so a pair of heavy, heat-resistant raku gloves would fit through them. The finished basket fit nicely into the raku kiln and could be lifted out of the kiln easily when it was loaded and hot. Always keep safety in mind when loading and firing a kiln. Now we can move onto the production process.

The jars were thrown with a smooth surface. After bisque firing to cone 07, they were gently sanded with a fine sandpaper to make the surface even smoother. This made the shape seem more visually appealing. The following steps allowed me to complete the task.

Recipes

Leach Porcelain

Grolleg Kaolin	53 %
Custer Feldspar	25
Silica (200 mesh)	20
Bentonite	2
	100 %

Peel-Away Slip

Fireclay	60 %
Kaolin	20
Silica	15
Grog (fine)	5
	100 %

Mix the slip to the consistency of pudding

Basket made with barbecue grill base and fencing bound together with #10 binding wire.

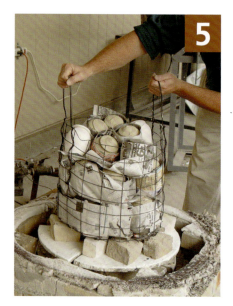

Coat the objects with a thick layer of the Peel-Away Slip. Make a thick slurry (about the consistency of pudding). Hold the covered jar (with lid attached), and rotate until it is covered in slip (figure 1).

Immediately place a piece of cut fiberglass screening around the object (figure 2). The fiberglass screening is available at any large lumber or hardware store, and it comes in various widths and is easy to cut.

Follow the fiberglass with a piece of newspaper wrapped in the same way (figure 3). This will protect the slip during the firing process.

Stack the jars in the wire basket until full (figure 4). They can touch since the newspaper protects them from each other.

Load the basket into the kiln and turn the burner on as if you were starting a raku firing (figure 5). Bring the temperature up slowly to about 1100°F (or until you just see color in the kiln).

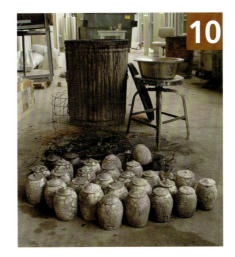

Shut the kiln off and (using protective equipment) carefully pull the whole basket from the kiln so that it can be placed in the reduction barrel (figure 6).

Place the basket into a barrel that has been prepared with a few pieces of newspaper in the bottom and around the sides to aid in the reduction process (figure 7).

Add some sawdust (figure 8) and cover the barrel for five minutes then remove the basket. Excess reduction can cause more gray areas. Shorter periods of time will allow the lines to be dark and crisp.

When the basket is cool, remove the pots. The fiberglass screening will come off easily, taking most of the Peel-Away Slip with it, exposing the beautiful large crackle effect underneath (figure 9). If the desired effects are not achieved, re-fire the pieces.

I could fire about 15 covered jars at a time and was able to finish the commission with results that I was proud of and that pleased the client (figure 10). I still have the basket and use it whenever I am making pieces with the Peel-Away Slip.

Horsehair Raku

by Bob Hasselle

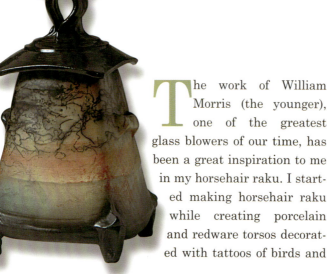

**"Pot with Necklace,"
16 inches in height,
handbuilt, with red
and white slip.**

The work of William Morris (the younger), one of the greatest glass blowers of our time, has been a great inspiration to me in my horsehair raku. I started making horsehair raku while creating porcelain and redware torsos decorated with tattoos of birds and animals. None of these works had the look that I was after, since the commercial look of clear glaze over red and white clay seemed to contradict the neolithic imagery. After setting them aside for about a year, I discovered the horsehair process, which gave them the overall look and surface patina that made them come alive.

**"Pot with Necklace,"
16 inches in height,
handbuilt, with red
and white slip.**

"Totem of the Salmon Cult," 17 inches in height.

The Horsehair Process

Applying horsehair is not a complicated process. Although I call my pots raku, because it is the category that fits best, they do not require the same level of heat. I take them out of the kiln at 1500°F by my pyrometer, which may not be accurate. I remove them when they are starting to glow inside of the pot. It's important to remember that you're not trying to melt glaze, only horsehair. The heat will determine the boldness of the black squiggles left by the horsehair. I like a bold line and darker effect. The hair from the tail of a horse is superior to the mane hair, because it is longer and more coarse.

Another tip for horsehair raku is to put some sawdust or other combustible under the bottom of the pot during firing. The temperature of the bottom of the pot is often not hot enough to ignite material after it comes out of the kiln. To get the brown to orange colors, spray the pot with ferric chloride after applying the horsehair.

In my work, I try to combine well-thought-out vessel shapes with very simplified sculptures of birds and animals reduced almost to gesture drawings in three dimensions. These sculptures are often wire cut from a block of clay to approximate dimensions. I then carve away and add clay until I get what I want. The finish can be attained with a hard-paste wax or sprayed on with polyurethane varnish, which can be tricky because it runs.

All kinds of pit and raku firing appeal to me, but if you want color control and a certain amount of compositional control, the horsehair raku process has its advantages. With this control, you can concentrate on the imagery and not worry whether

"Libido Fragment," 20 inches in height. Both are stoneware with kyanite added for thermal shock resistance, with Riggs Terra Sigillata, bisque fired to cone 07–06, then refired and removed from the kiln at cone 015 for horsehair application, by Bob Hasselle, Rock Hill, South Carolina.

that copper blush or carbon deposit will occur where you want it to.

I use underglazes for color before the bisque but after applying the terra sigillata. Terra sigillata allows one to polish the vessel to a near reflective surface. I recommend a recipe from Linda and Charlie Riggs. The quality of their work is a great standard to emulate.

Recipe

Riggs Terra Sigillata

Water	3½ gal
Sodium Silicate	1 tbsp
Soda Ash	1 tbsp
XX Saggar Clay	15 lbs

Mix ingredients and wait one day. Siphon off and use only the first 1½ gallons.

Hot-Wired
Wrapping Raku Pots with Wire

by Mark Gordon

I'm not sure what inspired me to crisscross copper wire for use as a surface treatment. Perhaps it was tying down cross-country truckloads under a tarp. Or the Japanese packaging illustrated in the book *How to Wrap Five Eggs*. Or maybe even my wife's all-consuming interest in crochet.

Whatever my inspiration, the result is an unpredictable skin shaped by the interplay of melting copper and molten glaze, influenced by heat variation and post-firing reduction in sawdust or straw.

Any clay body suitable for raku works for this process, but forms that have smoothly ribbed surfaces work best. Deep throwing rings can

distract from the flow of the pot's outer contour; and ridged forms seem to be less satisfying to wrap. Beyond the wheel-thrown-vessel format, there are endless possibilities.

Surface Preparation

After trimming your vessel, coat it with thick porcelain slip to promote strong chromatic contrast and color vibrancy. A slip-coated surface works well as long as it is a good fit with your clay body. After the piece is bisqued, you're ready to wrap wire.

Wire

The best wire is pure copper in a thickness of 32 or 26 gauge. I bought a few big rolls of surplus copper wire for $2 each in Des Moines, Iowa, in 1988. Before finding my Iowa wire bonanza, I used speaker wire stripped of its plastic coating, a labor-intensive method. (Don't burn coated wire; its fumes are potentially toxic.) Your best bet is using

Get copper wire at any hardware store; 32 and 26 gauge works well.

Cover the piece in slip and bisque fire. Then wrap the copper around the vessel. Be sure to go under and over, and have many cross-sections. Use square knots at the ends.

seven 17.5-foot-long pieces of wire. Larger vessels can readily accommodate 30-foot lengths of wire for each segment.)

Pass the wires underneath parts of the existing grid by prying with a thin knife. Use square knots to connect the wire segments. Overlapping and crossing the wires tends to tighten the mesh, an important precaution. Sometimes, loose wires can create a pleasant and unexpected effect, but more often they simply fall off.

Wrap the wire sparsely near the bottom of the vessel to prevent copper "foot melt," a technical imperfection that cannot easily be ground off low-temperature raku ware. You can wrap more densely near the top of the piece. Build your structure with relatively equal-distant crossed strands of wire. It's also a good idea to "counter wrap," or tie off, wherever wires cross. Be sure to counter-wrap and tie off a few times for each strand of wire. Perpendicular junctures are important to tighten and strengthen the whole wrap. If you're making a round vessel, watch the wire on the curves for signs of loosening during the wrapping. If this happens, use a few short lengths of wire to tie off separate wired areas of the vessel, pulling tighter with each knot and reducing looseness in the earlier wrapping. For "belted" shapes, wrap and tie extra layers of wire after initial wrapping, to help "cinch in" the wire toward the innermost curve. For a high-necked form, like the one seen here, wrap and rewrap the top "collar." The extra

copper craft wire or surplus wire used as internal coil wrapping for electric motors.

Wrapping

The process is simple enough. You want to wrap the vessel with copper wire, creating a wire mesh, then glaze and fire. During firing, the wire melts, forming an unpredictable surface pattern.

Start by choosing a length for the wire. Seek a balance; too long a wire is cumbersome; too short means you'll have to tie off a lot of pieces. A typical wire length is 15 to 20 feet. Shorter lengths are easier to handle, but require more connections (end ties); longer segments can be unwieldy. (The wide-mouth vessel shown here was completed with

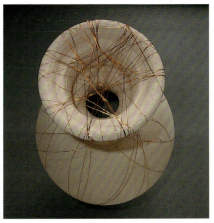

Wrap the top of the piece more densely than the bottom. This way the copper will not melt on the shelves, and no grinding will be needed. After the wire has been checked for kinks and is nice and taut, aqpply the glaze.

copper melts decoratively, descending downward onto the vessel walls. Now cross and recross your wire over the mouth of the piece; these can be coated in glaze also to melt into the vessel interior on firing.

Handle any kinks or tangles in the wire gingerly; sometimes it's best to cut loose any tangled sections of wire. If your wire breaks, find the

last place where you have 3 inches of free length, tie on a new wire and continue. Use small wire-cutting pliers to cut off any loose endsbefore glazing your piece.

Glazing

Brush your glaze on thickly by daubing and smoothing with brush strokes. Apply glaze extra thick over the wire, and even more over each wire knot. Keep the glaze near the bottom of your pieces significantly thinner to help prevent running.

If your wire becomes loose under the glaze, mix a small batch of glaze with common carpenter's glue (1 part glue and 3 parts glaze, by volume) and use this mixture as a preliminary coating. After the glaze/glue coating dries completely, apply another coat of glaze to build up thickness.

Firing and Post-Firing Reduction

I fire my kiln to cone 09, 1693°F on a standard thermocouple pyrometer. Keep in mind that every clay, glaze and wire combination will require different firing treatments.

A slow top-of-the-firing cycle helps promote a thorough melt and keeps the glaze from running from volatile copper wire. When cone 010 is bending, I use a 2-hour soak to promote evenness in the melt and to ensure that the wire is fully incorporated into the surface. To help absorb any minor glaze drips, softbrick can be used as a base during firing; the brick pad is easy to grind off if necessary.

Fire pieces to cone 09. A good soak will promote even melt of the copper wire. Remember, different clay and glazes require different firing temperatures and treatments. Fill a metal container with straw or shredded paper to act as a combustible to promote more patterning on the surface. Lay the piece in the container and sprinkle sawdust over the surface. Cover tightly, and let the pieces smoke until cool.

For surface variation, I use straw or shredded paper as a combustible for the carbonization. These materials contribute patterning to the copper-wire grid. Use a covered metal container filled with the straw and paper, with a shallow nest of sawdust on top. Place the foot of the superheated piece into the sawdust and sprinkle more sawdust thinly over the piece. Cover the container tightly with the metal lid. Leave the wire-wrapped pieces to smoke until cool.

Sometimes during the post-firing reduction, the molten copper wire migrates throughout the glaze, obliterating the linear patterning. Due to the inherent variation in this process, the wire-wrapping method can be unpredictable. In completing approximately 40 pieces using this method in 2004, my loss rate approached 25%.

Alternative Options

Bisque copper tubing or wire to 1500°F. Use a mortar and pestle to break off the calcined outer segments and grind them into flecks. Add the resulting copper flecks to any raku glaze. If you want a fairly smooth finished surface, screen out the larger pieces. Adding this rough granular calcined copper to stoneware glazes also can be interesting, especially on the insides of large bowls.

Brass wire, due to its high copper content, will respond much like copper in glazed raku. Iron wire often leaves a ghost impression or dark lines at raku temperatures, but has less chemical reaction than copper and will not normally melt into the glaze.

Where There's Smoke...
Testing Raku Combustibles

by Frank James Fisher

Raku firing dates back to sixteenth-century Japan. The Japanese tradition was based on an oxidized firing and cooling method. The introduction of a combustible reduction atmosphere is a recent North American development, and it's this process of doing something to a piece after it has been pulled from the fire that distinguishes Western raku from Japanese raku.

The most commonly used combustible for raku reduction is paper. I've used two types of paper—shredded office documents and shredded newspaper. My preference is newspaper because the colors in a luster glaze appear more intense and display greater color variety. This may be a result of the chemicals in the newspaper's printing inks.

Another common raku combustible is sawdust. Sawdust burns more like cinders in a fire, much slower than paper, and the areas of contact between the sawdust and the glaze surface often become speckled.

In considering other natural combustibles, such as leaves and grass clippings (two materials that I have too much of in my yard), I wondered how these materials would affect glaze color and surface. A side-by-side test to measure the differences would be an interesting project.

The Test

I began by throwing four similar spheres from white stoneware clay and bisque firing them. I selected Del Favero Luster as the glaze because it has a sensitive range of color depending on the post-firing reduction. I wiped each sphere with a damp sponge to remove any surface dust before glazing. Each sphere was dipped upside down to ⅓ of its height into a well-mixed bucket of Del Favero glaze. When dry, I loaded an airbrush with Del Favero Luster and sprayed a transition band along

**A glazed sphere
before raku firing.**

the longitude of the sphere. Again, I kept the glaze well mixed by shaking the airbrush's reservoir during the application. The sphere surface had both a thick, dipped application and a thin, sprayed application. The bottom third of the sphere was left bare (see above). This would provide a comparison of the carbonization on the surface.

With the glaze thoroughly dry, the four spheres were loaded into the raku kiln and fired to 1800°F. When

Placing sphere into a can of combustibles.

the glazed surface on the spheres appeared glassy, the kiln was turned off, the lid was removed, and, in quick succession, each sphere was rapidly pulled and placed into four separate, but identical, galvanized trashcans. Three cans were filled $2/3$ full with newspaper, grass clippings and leaves respectively, and a fourth can was filled half full of sawdust since the density of sawdust prevents the sphere from submerging into the combustible.

When each combustible burst into flames, we waited 10 seconds before sealing the can with the lid. The sawdust sphere also received a coating of sawdust to cover the top surface before the lid was sealed. The lids were reasonably tight and very little smoke escaped. We did not 'burp' the lid during reduction to re-ignite the combustibles. After an hour, the spheres had cooled down and each was removed. Under warm tap water, the surfaces were rinsed of any clinging, blackened combustible without scrubbing with a cleanser. After drying for a week, the four spheres were given a thin coat of sealer to bring out the blacks on the bare clay surface.

The Results

To say the least, I was shocked. The two main variables were the spontaneity of the combustible material and the amount of oxygen hidden within the layers of combustible. Both of these variables affected the strength of reduction occurring in each can.

Each sphere exhibited a very distinct look. If I hadn't experienced the test myself, I wouldn't have believed the variety of color in the results. The difference between the newspaper, the leaves and the sawdust was very dramatic. The grass clippings appeared to be a visual blend of the results seen using newspaper and leaves. The carbonization on the bare surfaces was virtually identical on all four spheres.

When I raku, newspaper remains my combustible of choice with an occasional handful of sawdust for added texture just before the can lid is sealed.

Recipe

Del Favero Luster

Gerstley Borate	80 %
Cornwall Stone	20
	100 %
Add: Copper Carbonate	2 %

Del Favero Luster settles very quickly, so it's important to remix the glaze preceding each dip.

Shredded Newspaper

I understand why newspaper is a preferred combustible choice—very strong reduction. Paper burns rapidly upon contact with the fired clay surface. The quicker ignition removes the oxygen rapidly from the air providing a strong reduction atmosphere. Less oxygen results in flashes of red from the copper in the glaze. Paper is a flexible material and compresses easily allowing a lot of paper to be packed into a can for a maximum oxygen burn-off. The paper left minimal markings on the final glaze surface. The surface showed no discernible difference between the thick and thin applications of glaze, and nearly all the paper that was in the can was ignited.

Sawdust

The sawdust sphere had a very strong reduction and an interesting speckled texture on the glaze surface. Each dot of black represented burned sawdust. The sphere was buried halfway into the sawdust. The upper surface was then covered with additional sawdust leaving no exposed glaze surface to receive oxygen. Had the surface of the glaze been exposed to oxygen, a very different outcome would have resulted. The surface showed no discernible difference between the thick and thin applications of glaze. The sawdust in the can that came in contact with the sphere surface ignited while the remaining sawdust was virtually untouched. A stiff brush was needed to dislodge the cindered sawdust from the glaze surface.

Dry Leaves

The leaves had minimal effect on reduction. The dry leaves were stiff and did not compress as readily as the newspaper, and there were pockets of oxygen, more than the other combustibles tested. During reduction, the availability of oxygen caused the copper to turn green. The leaves did not burst into flames with the same intensity as the newspaper; instead, it was more of a gradual build, igniting approximately half of the leaves. Leaves are similar to paper regarding surface contact—virtually no affect on the glazed surface. The glaze displayed a green mottling on the thick application but not on the thin application. Slight reduction occurred near the bottom of the sphere on the glazed areas. This is a result of the weight of the sphere pressing into the leaves and smothering out the oxygen.

Grass Clippings

The can filled with grass clippings provided a varied reduction. Some of the surface had a smoky bronze coloring and other areas had a green/white surface similar to the leaves. The grass clippings were reasonably dry, but did not ignite readily like the newspaper. It was more of a slow, smoldering burn with flames clearly visible, igniting approximately half of the grass clippings. Because the grass clippings did not burn readily, oxygen was not quickly consumed. The smoke was very heavy and thick, and may have contributed to the vertical areas of dark reduction up the side of the sphere. The glaze surface displayed a distinct green mottling on the thick glaze application but not on the thin application. The burning grass left a few black dashes on the glaze surface.

Lisa Merida-Paytes
Cutting to the Bone

by Steve Kissing

"Frozen Fish II on Granite," 30 inches in height, with copper wire and granite. This white raku piece was coil built and brushed with three coats of White Crackle Glaze, which was then wiped off the surface. It was then raku fired with post-fire reduction in sawdust and straw.

It would be a gross understatement to say that Lisa Merida-Paytes had an unusual childhood. After all, how many of us grew up amidst the sights, sounds and smells of a home-based business built upon death and dismemberment? Perhaps you're guessing Merida-Paytes had a "Sopranos" or "Six Feet Under" sort of upbringing. But her father's business was neither illegal nor the kind you associate with a hearse. His business was about—depending on your point of view—either the destruction or preservation of nature: taxidermy.

"The most powerful image that stays with me is coming home with a friend or a date during deer season," says Merida-Paytes, who grew up in Verona, Kentucky, thirty miles south of Cincinnati. "I remember the driveway filled with gun-toting hunters standing proudly next to their fresh kills. My dad hung their deer upside-down to make it easy for him to cut away anything that got in the way of a perfect pelt. As a result, dad always had piles of skinless deer legs and feet laying in our yard."

Merida-Paytes does manage to find some humor and lighter moments growing up in what most would consider a surreal environment; one with freezers full of animal hides, cutting and skinning tools scattered throughout the home, and skinned raccoons, squirrels and groundhogs floating in pans of saltwater in the refrigerator—that night's dinner.

"Over the years, my dad's business grew so much that he needed more room to prepare hides, mount animals and such," she says. "We didn't have much money, so it made more sense to convert our family room into another workshop. It was very strange to eat birthday cake with your friends while mounted animal heads hovered above you, their unblinking eyes studying you from every angle."

Is it any wonder, then, that Merida-Paytes suggests her art is an exploration of her father's traditions and its unsettling subject matter and disregard for life? Of course not. Just as her desire to "expose the unseen core, the essential structure of skeletal or embryonic animal references" is also obvious in her work. Painfully so, some would argue.

Yet, it's not anger or bitterness that seems to drive Merida-Paytes, a petite, happy, mother of two. Merida-Paytes seems to have come to terms with the craft and traditions of taxidermy that helped to feed and form her, in part because they still do. But she also strives to distance herself existentially, via her art, from some aspects of her unconventional upbringing.

"The intent of my work is to evoke the animal spirits that were destroyed, and to make amends for that discord and waste," she says, her eyes gleaming with sadness and sincerity. "By uncovering the strength and beauty in frailty, I hope to leave viewers with a greater appreciation and respect for life."

In 1991, Merida-Paytes graduated with a B.F.A. from the Art Academy of Cincinnati. At that point in her artistic development, she was focused on creating large, site-specific environmental sculptures, sometimes with welded or wooden internal structures. She had applied to several graduate programs around the country and was accepted into the prestigious Cranbook Graduate School in Bloomfield, Michigan. However, shortly before earning her bachelor's degree, she was involved in a horrific car accident. A driver ran a red light and struck Merida-Paytes' car, totaling her vehicle, and performing quite the number on her back and neck. Her doctor ordered a 24-hour morphine drip to ease the pain and to speed her initial recovery so she could begin intensive therapy.

"It was difficult and painful just to raise my arms above my head, to stay sitting for any period of time and even to simply hold or lift an object," says Merida-Paytes, with a look of remembered pain and frustration on her face. "That period was the worst time in my life. I could not attend Cranbrook, my dream." There was a pregnant pause before Merida-Paytes uttered every artist's deepest fear, the one that pains us even to think about: "I could not create my art."

But like her ceramic sculptures that are transformed and made beautiful by their time in the kiln, Merida-Paytes, too, would emerge better from her time confined in and fired by a metaphorical kiln. In fact, her personal metamorphosis rivals, if not supersedes, the beauty and wonder of her art.

While recovering from her injuries and trying her best to manage the pain and frustration of having her art—her identity—sitting teasingly just beyond her reach, Merida-Paytes sought mental refuge; a means of distracting herself from the heartache of her situation. So, she bought a bag of clay to strengthen the muscles in her back and neck, but perhaps more importantly, to keep her hands moving; anything for a sense, however fleeting, of moving forward; a sense of healing; a sense of sculpting.

"When I began working with this new material, I was amazed with the options that I had, technically and aesthetically," Merida-Paytes says. "I began to explore the possibilities of clay and started seeking out anyone who worked with the material, including potters and ceramic suppliers. And I read books, lots and lots of books." She also found inspiration—and still does—in such contemporary artists as Martin Puryear and his dynamic form; Stephen DeStaebler's massive, rough-textured sculptures; Viola Frey's rich, tactile surfaces; and Mary Frank's novel uses of clay.

Merida-Paytes says she quickly realized there was so much technical information to digest in order to fulfill her vision that she decided she needed a more focused, intensive period of study. It took five years of recovery before she began to feel better. But once she emerged from her personal crucible, among her first major decisions was applying to the

"Fish Stringer V," 48 inches in height, with wood and chain. Each fish is coil-built and carved white raku clay. They were brushed with three coats of White Crackle and Copper Matt Raku glazes, which were then wiped off the surface. They were then raku fired with post-fire reduction in sawdust, straw and leaves.

University of Cincinnati's fine arts graduate program. She was quickly accepted and began to study under professor Roy Cartwright, a nationally known potter and sculptor who to this day remains a mentor to Merida-Paytes. "He welcomed me into his department with open arms and a contagious enthusiasm," says Merida-Paytes. "I became a sponge, learning everything I could from him and my peers about materials, form and technique." She graduated with an M.F.A. in ceramic sculpture.

Merida-Paytes currently teaches students of all ages and skill levels at her studio, what she calls the "art shack," which is situated behind her two-story home, where her husband, Sean, runs a hair salon on the first floor. (Merida-Paytes says Sean, a master hair colorist, often gives invaluable advice about color, hue and density.) Merida-Paytes is also on the school of art faculty at the University of Cincinnati.

Despite her accomplishments, Merida-Paytes still sees herself in the early stages of her new artistic journey, one that began with twisted metal and an ambulance ride. "I'm just beginning to understand clay's inherent possibilities," she says. "I still get giddy when 'happy accidents' occur."

One such happy accident occurred two years ago, injecting yet more irony, more poetry—and perhaps more evidence of divine providence—into Merida-Paytes' life. A few years ago, she and her family, including her parents, made a road trip to Panama

City, Florida. "We were almost to our rented condo when we spotted a small roadside stand with fresh fruits, so we stopped," says Merida-Paytes. "We all got out to stretch our legs and to buy fruit, and then I saw it!"

"It" was a football-sized blowfish hanging above the oranges, a blowfish that was clearly mounted by an accomplished taxidermist. The fine stitching on its back and its faux, yet inquisitive eyes gave it away. Merida-Paytes says that the fish embodied so many characteristics that she had been exploring on her own, both in terms of method and form. "Specifically," she says, "that blowfish contained beautiful, inherent texture and color. But it wasn't secondary to its form. Its entire body had almost a skeletal, transparent skin."

After settling back at home with the blowfish—which still hangs in her studio—Merida-Paytes began conducting many tests with porcelain, porcelain slip, fiberglass cloth and various gauges of steel to emulate the characteristics of the blowfish's body and fins.

"These sculptures contain handbuilt and extruded areas throughout the forms in conjunction with areas that contain fiberglass, burlap, and cheesecloth coated in porcelain slip," Merida-Paytes explains. "The combustible material burns out in the kiln and leaves slip-covered areas, which allude to a transparent skin."

This work, supported by an Ohio Arts Council grant, became

"Arthritis," 19 inches in height, coil-built white raku clay, fired to cone 05, by Lisa Merida-Paytes, Cincinnati, Ohio. Merida-Paytes states that referencing animal structures helps her understand her own growth and decay.

the basis for a year-long investigation into material, process, design and self-expression. It's remarkable to think that so much inspiration, experimentation and imagination came from one serendipitous encounter—with a fish no less.

But the most beautiful element of the Florida story is how the blowfish made its way back home with Merida-Paytes. During the tedious thirteen-hour drive home, Merida-Paytes' delicate aquatic treasure—a creature frozen in time thanks to the patient skills of a taxidermist—sat on her father's lap. The very man who had been a co-conspirator in the death of so many animals, was now aiding and abetting a new approach to art, to life.

Merida-Paytes' father held the blowfish protectively for all 900 miles up Interstate 75, the highway that runs right by their hometown. There, the deer still can't escape the hunters' bullets. And there, like everywhere, people still can't escape the tough and unsettling lessons of life and death; the very lessons that inspire so much art and make it so joyful—and at times heartbreaking—to encounter.

Recipes

Copper Matt Raku
Cone 010–06

Bone Ash.	33 %
Gerstley Borate	67
	100 %
Add: Copper Carbonate.	8 %
Cobalt Carbonate	2 %

Remarkably, this versatile glaze is capable of producing a wide range of colors that are very receptive to atmospheric changes inside the kiln and outside in post-fire reduction. Through experimenting with the application of this glaze, I have been able to achieve a beautiful mottled surface with striking luster and opalescent color. I have found that applying less is better—one thin coat then wiping the glaze off with a dry towel works best to achieve a matt, speckled surface.

White Crackle Raku
Cone 010–06

Barium Carbonate	15 %
Gerstley Borate	40
Nepheline Syenite	35
Silica	10
	100 %

George Whitten
Icons and Artifacts

by Bob Hasselle

Drape-molded platter with wheel-thrown foot, approximately 15 inches in diameter, multifired.

An unassuming man, George Whitten lives an almost hermitlike lifestyle, although when he does have guests, he is the life of the party. He has worked very hard to develop his raku process and, until now, has not been too interested in sharing it with the world at large. This is not to say that Whitten's work has been unappreciated. His name may not be a buzzword on the lecture circuit, although he has done his share of workshops, but his work has not escaped the notice of New York interior designers and collectors.

This has not happened by accident. In the commercial sphere, Whitten has been a tireless promoter of his own work. I encountered an example of this while at an American Crafts Council show in Chicago. When a buyer from American Artisans in Sherman Oaks, California, stopped by to place an order, I happened to mention George Whitten. She told me he used to show up at her gallery with a whole van full of raku pots, and let her pick out what she wanted. Later, I mentioned to Whitten that Sherman Oaks was a helluva drive from Mansfield, Ohio, just to make a cold call! He replied that back in the 1980s he used to do that kind of marketing all the time; many times the first gallery he called on would buy the whole truckload just to keep them out of the hands of competitors.

His work was particularly hot in the '80s: Whitten pots were featured in several movies and television shows. An interior design showroom

Ohio potter George Whitten uses templates to construct "blank" forms to be altered in different ways.

in Miami that handled his work had an arrangement with the *Miami Vice* television series. It was basically a rental agreement, with an understanding that if the piece was broken in a fight scene or machine gun episode, it was upgraded from rental to purchase.

Whitten started off making pots with David Tell at Florida Atlantic University. He stayed after graduation to learn more about ceramics. Finally, Tell told him that he was ready for graduate school, and even arranged interviews for him at three. Whitten ended up going to Wichita State.

After graduating in 1974, he accepted a teaching job at Ohio University in Athens. He stopped off in the vicinity of Mansfield to spend part of the summer with friends. By the time he got to Athens, the Arab oil embargo was in full swing, and the job had been eliminated due to budget cuts. The school had tried to reach him over the summer, but couldn't locate him.

So Whitten went back to the Amish country east of Mansfield, with the idea of establishing a studio. This plan never materialized; instead, he hooked up with three friends in the Mansfield area and together they started a co-op pottery. A sympathetic farmer outside the village of Mifflin, Ohio, provided an outbuilding, which they fixed up as a studio. A few years later, after the other three potters had moved on and the farmer announced he was ready to retire, Whitten bought the place and

has since operated it independently.

The first thing about his place that impresses the visitor is the total sense of privacy. There is a long driveway that drops down from the road into the 40-acre spread, which includes a number of outbuildings of dubious use and vintage. There is even another house on the property, which Whitten rents out. It's quiet now, but a few years ago the place was somewhat busier, with potters Tim Mather and Annette McCormick working in one of the outbuildings and four or five apprentices working for Whitten in the main studio.

The studio is a little drafty by urban standards, but has lots of space and a good division of extra rooms for the dirty work. In addition to his wheel work, Whitten produces drape-molded platters to which a thrown foot is added. Most of the slab pieces are begun by apprentices; cardboard templates are used to cut out the walls, which are textured and brushed with slip while still flat. The apprentice scores the edges and assembles the shapes, then Whitten does the final alterations. He considers these basic forms to be blank canvases, which he alters and glazes in totally different ways; however, the size and general shapes remain constant, which allows enough continuity to satisfy wholesale customers.

Whitten began rakuing in 1979, when he decided to give up salt glazing—and almost gave up pottery as well. His plans were vague, but he was leaning toward becoming a truck driver. He had a few hundred

Raku basket, approximately 12 inches in height, assembled from template-cut slabs, then manipulated and textured, with multiple terra sigillatas and glazes.

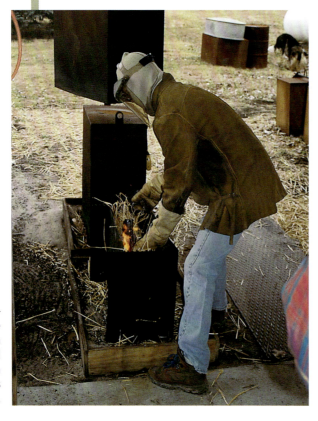

The 1500°–1600°F piece is placed in a "chimney" filled with straw, then more straw is thrown on top.

Recipes

Whitten Sculpture Body
Cone 10

F-I Wollastonite	10 lb
6-Tile Clay.	25
EPK Kaolin.	50
Kentucky Ball Clay (OM 4)	25
Kyanite (35 mesh)	20
Extra-fine Grog	10
Fine Grog	10
Medium Grog	10
	160 lb

Whitten Throwing Body
Cone 10

F-I Wollastonite	10 lb
6-Tile Clay.	50
Kentucky Ball Clay (OM 4)	25
Kyanite (35 mesh)	20
Extra-fine Grog	20
Fine Grog	10
	135 lb

George Whitten Copper Matt
Cone 05

White Lead Bisilicate	9.5%
Frit 3110 (Ferro)	7.6
Iron Oxide.	1.9
Red Copper Oxide	76.2
Veegum T	4.8
	100.0%

pounds of clay left and decided to make some raku pieces for himself.

Whitten is very proud of his raku bodies. He is able to produce pieces up to 4 feet in height, and has taken some of them through the raku process as many as 25 times without cracking. Because of variations in mined clays, especially the fireclays, he has tried to stick with more refined ingredients; all of the grogs are manufactured by North American Refractory.

Before mixing either body, stir the wollastonite in water, then screen. Both clay bodies are suitable for a variety of situations and will go up to cone 10 without deformation. Though fairly expensive to make,

they are practically immune to thermal shock.

Whitten's glaze firings are done in electric kilns. He applies many layers of colored terra sigillatas (mixed with frit or borax to help resist the smoke) and low-fire glazes; all are fired before the copper matt finish is applied. Even the copper matt is prefired to cone 05 before the pot is rakued.

For a white crackle and general-purpose base glaze, Whitten uses a commercial clear (Gare 1700). A vat of this glaze in watered-down form is also sometimes used as a thin wash underneath the copper matt.

His copper matt glaze is applied thinner than most stoneware glazes, but much thicker than the thin washes a lot of raku potters use. He likes it to develop a little sheen, and says that his glazes are more color-fast because of this and the cone 05 firing.

Mix with 2 pints vinegar; the vinegar is not an active ingredient, but is used to break the surface tension and allow dispersion of the copper. Epsom salts may be added to prevent settling. Be sure to take all safety precautions when handling the raw ingredients and fire in a well-ventilated kiln. Do not use on surfaces that may come in contact with food or beverages.

As mentioned before, each piece is fired more than once to cone 05. This matures the copper matt and the other glazes before the raku firing. Then the raku firing process is varied according to the results desired. For example, the white crackle with colored slips is taken out of the kiln at 1200°–1400°F, placed in an open container filled with straw, and covered with more straw. The container is left open, and the smoke turns the crackle patterns black.

A hoist allows Whitten to easily lower and raise the heavy metal lid.

The copper matts are handled in a totally different way. Whitten uses a sand pit with what he calls a "chimney." This is a metal box with holes drilled in it and notches welded on the inside for altering the size of the chamber. The chimney is packed with straw, and the piece is fired to about 1800°F. When it cools down to 1500°–1600°F, it is removed from the kiln by gloved hand, or if it has a handle, by a metal bar, and is placed in the chimney. A small handful of sawdust mixed with kerosene is thrown into the container to ensure instantaneous combustion. The heavy metal lid is lowered down over the piece by hoist and is forced into the sand.

Raku teapot, 12 inches
in height.

Covered jar, approximate-
ly 10 inches in height,
by George Whitten,
Mansfield, Ohio.

Some pieces are made in sections so that they can incorporate differently treated sections; e.g., copper matt with white crackle parts.

Altogether, Whitten's work offers a panoply of forms, textures and colors. Back in the 1980s, I went to a show of works by raku potter Rick Foris with my friend Prue Warren. She described Foris' work as classical artifacts, but of a culture just not found on this planet. Whitten's work sometimes exhibits this kind of radical originality, especially in the thrown pieces, decorating techniques and alterations. The large slab vessels, however, are another matter. They seem to be icons, effortlessly spanning the gap between postmodern Western art and a kind of Zen-flavored orientalism. They look equally like artifacts from some distant past and time travelers from the future.

The Golden Touch
Enhancing Raku with Lusters

by John Martin

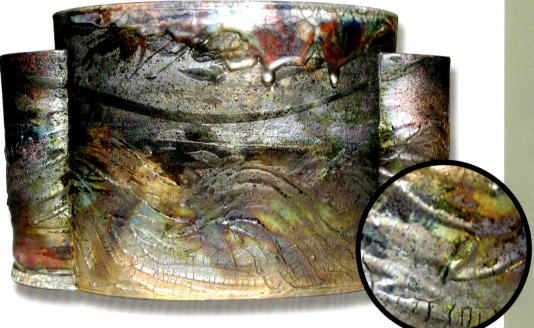

"Raku Floral Form,"
19 inches in length.
Thrown and assembled
with applied vitreous
slip texture, colored
slips and lusters ap-
plied at various stages.
Multiple firings ending
with raku post-firing
reduction.

Detail showing effects
of crackled surface,
multiple colored glaz-
es and lusters after
post-firing reduction.

There's a renaissance in raku occurring with the advancements and availability of new colors. New technologies have allowed the potter to buy ready-to-use pre-made colors. Stains and gold lusters have become a more consistent and durable means of infusing a surface with saturated color. Different stains can be mixed together just like mixing paint. This allows a potter to have an unlimited palette rich in color, while maintaining the atmospheric quality and crackle of raku.

With commercial lusters, the glazed form records the memory of the fire. Gold luster flashes in the raku reduction, extending its range of character while creating beautiful transitions of color that reflect light. The real secret to using lusters effectively is knowing how to develop the glazed and unglazed surfaces underneath.

By building up the surface quality with vitreous slips, copper accents and glossy glaze the harmony of the gold is balanced by the opportunity for spontaneous variation.

The lusters are applied outdoors with an airbrush using both red and yellow gold. The vessel is then fired in an outdoor electric kiln to cone 019. After cooling, a thin coat of opal is applied. The thin wash of opal creates a rainbow of color, so a light overspray in areas enhances the flash of the fire.

The final firing at cone 021 is sufficient red heat to create an intersection of carbon transfer, good crackle, copper flash and gold flash.

Recipes

Vitreous Stretch Slip

Ferro Frit 3134	30 %
EPK Kaolin	70
	100 %

Shiny White Crackle

Cone 06

Ferro Frit 3134	70 %
EPK kaolin	30
	100 %
Add: Gum	2 %

To get intense colors, add 30% of the following stains to this glaze. All the stains are Mason stains unless otherwise noted.

6121 Saturn Orange
6129 Golden Ambrosia
6207 Tangerine
6343 Mediterranean Blue
6378 Cerulean Blue
6381 Blackberry Wine
6404 Vanadium Yellow
6319 Lavender
Bordeaux Red 44769 (Cerdec)
Intense Red 44768 (Cerdec)

Copper Accent

Cone 06

Copper Carbonate	70 %
Borax	30
	100 %
Add: Gum	3 %

Jade

Cone 06

Ferro Frit 3134	70 %
EPK Kaolin	30
	100 %
Add: Copper Carbonate	2 %
Gum	2 %

Lusters

Engelhard N-Gold: Fire to cone 019
Engelhard Luster Gold 170: Fire to cone 019
Engelhard Opal 850: Final firing at cone 021

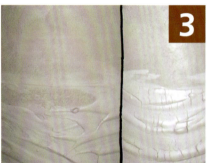

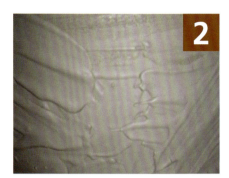

To get a heavily textured surface, apply slip to the outside of a freshly thrown form (figure 1). The slip should be thick enough to create a variey of textures without running.

Use a torch to dry the slip until it's no longer shiny and starts to crackle (figure 2). The crackle is enhanced by stretching the clay using a wooden rib on the inside.

After the clay reaches leather hard, construction is completed (figure 3). Here I've taken a cylinder, cut it in half, attached it to the sides and added caps

After bisque firing to cone 04, pour glaze into the piece and work quickly to roll it around (figure 4). Rotate the piece as you pour out the glaze to evenly coat the rim.

To highlight the texture, brush White Crackle glaze over the vitreous slip (figure 5). Next, sponge away the surface to leave glaze in the low areas and cracks.

Apply white glaze with a slip trailer (figure 6) and bamboo brush, then start to add colors. I often overlap up to five coats. Slip trailing white over the pattern adds even more movement.

Brush copper accents onto the unglazed areas and the vitreous slip (figure 7). Splatter more white glaze over the exterior using a scrubbing brush and fire to cone 06.

Apply liquid N-Gold luster with an airbrush over the copper accents, then apply Gold 170 over remaining areas of slip stopping just below the edge of the glazed surface (figure 8).

Fire the piece to cone 019, then spray the lusters with a thin coat of Opal (figure 9).

Fill a can halfway with dry sawdust then line the perimeter with newsprint (figure 10). Fire the piece to cone 021 and remove it hot. Light the paper and place the piece into a metal trash can of burning sawdust and newsprint. The preheated environment reduces thermal shock and unnecessary cracking.

Pour in more sawdust and add more newsprint to establish a blazing fire and add to the insulation in the cooling period (figure 11).

WARNING

When spraying lusters, it's very important to use a NIOSH/MSHA approved respirator with an organic vapor cartridge that blocks or removes vapors. I use an inline air hood that delivers fresh air through a hose.

Art on the Wall
Making a Raku Mural

by Barbara VanSickle

"White Pines," 24 inches in height.

The idea of creating raku murals happened quite naturally. A few years ago I was fortunate enough to be asked to create a retirement gift for a dear friend and former colleague. I needed to design something very special. I knew that he was partial to raku surfaces. During visits to his home, I was struck by its impressive open-concept architecture with the tall, wide wall spaces. The more I thought about what to make, the clearer it became: a raku mural.

The problem was I had no idea on how to proceed. My experience with raku was limited and, although I had previously created some murals for a school installation with children, I'd never attempted anything like this. The school project gave me some of the technical knowledge and experience of creating, drying and mounting the clay tiles but I needed inspiration for the subject matter.

I turned to my own environment and my love of Art Nouveau stained glass to come up with the design for "India Blue Peacock." Two doors down the road from me lives a family that raises India Blues. I hear the peacock calls all through the days from early spring to late fall. Linking the peacock with the Art Nouveau stained-glass look was quite natural.

Since making this first mural, I have continued to look to my own experiences and environment for inspiration.

Prepare Paper Template

Begin a mural by making a series of small drawings. Whatever your inspiration, remember that simplified edges work best (as in stained glass) and that some areas naturally lend themselves to being cut into sections. If you have areas that would be too large for one tile, plan how you'll adapt your work by adding divisions in the tiles that add to the overall de-

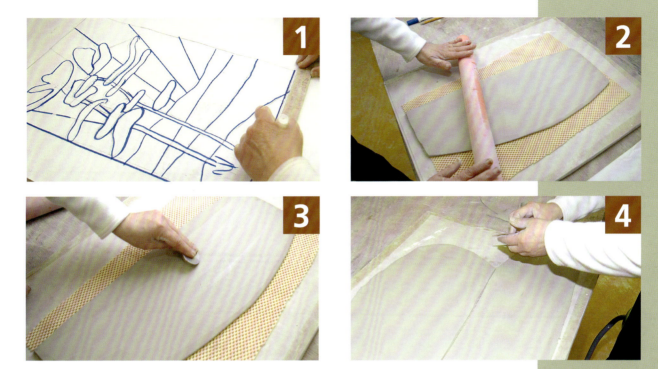

sign. Enlarge the drawing to actual size, then use a marker to highlight the lines. On larger projects, you'll need to cut your plan into smaller pieces. If so, number each piece on the back to make it easier to reassemble later (figure 1).

Prepare the Slab

Roll out a slab to a thickness of approximately ⅜ inch on a textured material, such as rubber shelf liner or placemats. The textured rubber material provides a perfect backing for the tile, which helps prevent warping during drying and firing. It also makes the slabs easy to carry without distorting (figure 2). Remove any unwanted marks with a rib and rolling pin, being sure to roll the slab no thinner than ⅓ inch. Thinner tiles are more likely to warp during drying and firing (figure 3). Peel off the

rubber backing, then join slabs together as needed (figure 4). Place the slabs on a flat surface, and cover it with plastic for about a day.

Transfer the Design

Lay the paper pattern on the slab, then using a blunt tool, such as the dull end of a wooden skewer, trace over the marker lines. When the template is removed, you will be able to use the incised lines as guides for adding any relief or textures. Trim the edges of your panel using a straightedge and a sharp, dry knife, then cut the panel into individual tiles (figure 5).

Create the Pieces

Arrange your cut tiles on a large board or table to form your mural and add any relief or impressed designs. Once you've completed all the

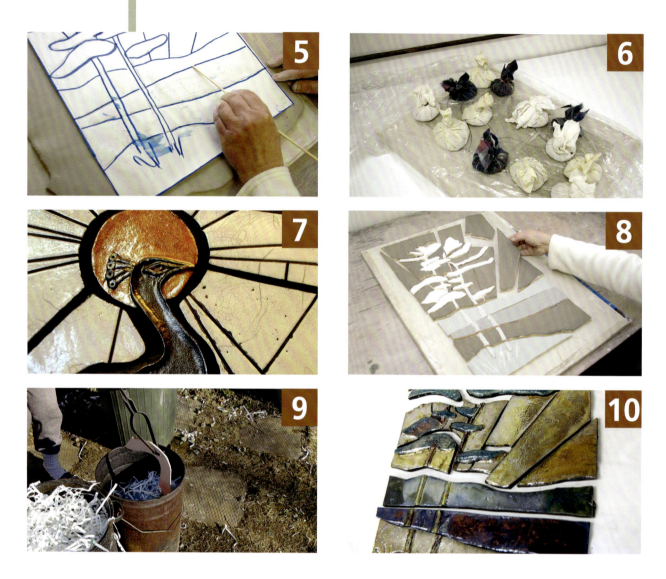

additions, cut through any pieces that overlap from tile to tile. Clean up and smooth all edges.

Drying process

Cover the entire mural with plastic, and place sandbags strategically to keep the pieces as flat as possible during the drying phase. Tip: I make sandbags by cutting up old sheets into 12-inch squares, then scoop sand onto them, bring the edges up and fasten them with rubber bands. They are a great tool to have around the studio (figure 6). Check on the mural daily as warping can be reduced by relocating the sandbags if you catch it right away. Once leather hard, turn the tiles over and recover with plastic to allow them to dry slowly (about a week in my studio). Remove the plastic, turn the tiles right side up, and give the work at least another day to dry before bisque firing.

Glazing

Reassemble all the pieces to form the mural before glazing. This makes it much easier to apply the glazes accurately. If you're masking any areas, apply your tape or resist material. I prefer to use black graphic tape as it provides excellent contrast, and can easily be rearranged without leaving residue on the bisqued tiles. It also creates perfectly straight lines (figure 7). Apply glazes according to your original drawings. I prefer to brush them on by completing all of one glaze color at a time on the entire mural before moving to the next glaze (figure 8).

Raku

I fire my mural pieces in a raku kiln (figure 9). Due to the extreme range of reduction effects that influence the glaze surface and color development, try to fire tiles that will be side by side in the mural in the same load. If possible place them in the same reduction chamber together. Use a pyrometer and time each fire to get the greatest consistency between loads, and try to fire under the same conditions if your work will take longer than a day. This process takes considerable planning but the results are well worth the effort. If you get too much or too little reduc-

"The Three Sisters,"
22 inches in height, raku fired,
by Barbara Vansickle.

"India Blue Peacock," 48 inches
in height.

tion on a particular piece, remember that you can always refire.

Assemble the mural

Reassemble the mural (figure 10) and measure the finished height and width. This is the base measurement for your mounting board. Where and how your work is hung determines the type of material for mounting. If you're working on a project any larger that 8 square feet, use plywood. For smaller murals, I recommend ⅝-inch-thick medium density fiber board (MDF) as it is lighter, though on larger murals it can warp.

For a mural the size made here, mark the MDF board roughly three-fourths of the way up from the bottom edge and drill ¼-inch holes 2 inches in from either side. Countersink the holes on the front of the board deep enough for a ¼-inch nut to be flush with the face. Drill two large diameter washers to accept the hanging wire and bend them slightly outward. Attach the washers to the back of the board through the ¼-inch bolt head and tighten (figure 11).

Prime the MDF and, when thoroughly dry, apply paint (I prefer matt black). Allow the paint to dry completely for 24 hours, then spread a good quality construction glue to the mounting board, keeping it off anywhere that will show when done (figure 12). Beginning at the bottom, apply the glue to the back of the tiles, one or two at a time, and assemble. The glue dries very fast, so you'll need to work quickly (figure 13).

When it is completely dry (at least 8 hours), grout the mural. Remember in your planning that grout comes in many colors so it can further enhance the final project. Follow the manufacturer's instructions. Once the grout begins to thicken, pour it on the mural paying particular attention to the small spaces between each tile (figure 14). Gradually remove the extra grout using a damp sponge, changing the water frequently (figure 15). Allow to dry.

Thread heavy duty picture wire through the holes in the washers and adjust the length appropriately.

Breaking Through to Familiar Ground

by Frank James Fisher

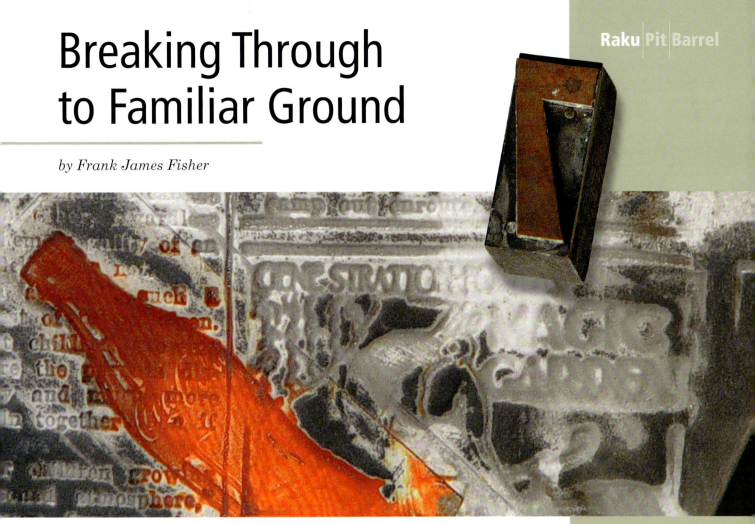

Detail of "High Protein Drink," slab-built porcelain, raku fired, 2005. "My graphic series is a culmination of my advertising experience. I have a professional eye for graphics and a love for ceramics. This marriage of two-dimensional graphic design applied to three-dimensional design is the heart and soul of my art. The artwork takes the advertising and communication images of American culture and applies them to anything and everything. Newspapers, advertisements, packaging, promotional flyers, logos, photos all become elements of design," says Fisher.

I t is not easy to be an artist. It is enjoyable and gratifying, but definitely not easy. That's why success tastes so sweet when we reach our goals. Goals in this instance are artistic accomplishments or milestones; a point of departure that signals something creative and new has developed.

Developing your artistic voice can be a complicated journey. We all have our favorite artists. We admire their work and dream of creating works of that caliber. Our first period of creative development is spent imitating

artistic heroes. We become disciples of their style. Then, a crucial moment arrives and we begin to break from our hero's influence to explore new ground of our own. Sometimes, we embrace yet another artist and follow in his or her footsteps.

This was my plight; many years of imitating the voices of other artists. And I knew it too. I had sidetracked my artistic evolution by looking to the art of others to find myself.

My difficulty began when I poured my best creative energy into my day job as a creative director in Detroit's

"War," 11 inches in height, slab-built porcelain, raku fired, with cord, 2006. "To create these [graphic] works, I have accumulated a library of discarded printing plates to mark the clay with impressions," states Fisher.

"Some Tea and the Latest News," 7½ inches in height, thrown and slab-built porcelain, raku fired, 2004.

advertising community. By evening, my creativity was too exhausted to develop a personal artistic expression of my own. There is little common ground between advertising and fine art. In art school, my generation was reminded that commercial artists were not real artists. As an aspiring fine artist, this meant my forty hours a week of creative experiences needed to be abandoned. In fact, to be a real artist, I needed to erase those influences and move 180° in the opposite direction, wherever that might be. That became the puzzle. I needed to deny myself to be myself.

Every craft has a set of guidelines to assist with your creative approach. In advertising, your guidelines involve white space, headlines, tag lines, body text, logos, key graphics and spot colors to name a few. These are the tools of the trade. At work I immersed myself in these tools until I owned them. I knew every variation they could produce. Imagine the frustration of introducing these commercial tools into a natural medium like clay. I couldn't create because my mind was aligned to advertising. For clay, my brain required an entirely different set of aesthetics, a naturally inspired set. How could I explore clay with a headline or squeeze in a strong graphic element with supporting text?

My unoriginal solution was to imitate the style of other ceramics artists. But the works I created were not truly mine. Each was an imitation. The art looked wonderful, but it did not give me a deep personal satisfaction. An artist arrives at their artistic style or voice through personal experience. I had attempted to bypass that experience. I skipped the previous steps the artist experienced, so it was difficult to move forward. It felt like I was writing a novel at the halfway mark, not having read the first half, and not having a clue as to the next page. The sequence of design was gone. It would never be my novel. There is a positive side to this long study period; I became extremely accomplished in a diverse range of methods, styles and mediums. On the negative side, I had not moved any closer to creating my own art.

In 2002, I took the first step in my own direction. I began a series of ceramic teapots that were inspired by a fascination with industrial fixtures and containers. Manufacturing shapes speak with an honest sense of function and purpose. My fascination was the result of researching and photographing manufacturing facilities for numerous advertising and promotional materials. I created imaginary gas cans by applying my graphic and package design knowledge to the clay. In the true spirit of American marketing, I called them Tea-Cans. Through trial and error, I gravitated to raku firing and evolved a unique glazing process to capture a gritty graphic quality on the clay surface. The result was a purely nostalgic, American vessel.

With the new direction my art had taken, I stopped imitating and began exploring and inventing solutions to concepts I could only visualize. For example, when the clay needed to resemble weathered, thin, galvanized metal, I experimented until that look was accomplished. My thinking moved beyond the clay in terms of the final artwork. The realization took hold that my artwork did not need to be similar to another artists' work to be successful, it only needed to match my vision of art. And my vision revolved around the graphic language of commercial art. This took too many years to realize and embrace. Commercial art could be applied to fine art.

One evening, I watched a television program that featured archaeologists learning about an ancient culture through the study of pottery shards. I tried to imagine modern ceramics as a heightened representation of the current American culture. America is a communication-based country like no other place in the world. Nearly everything we produce is wrapped in logos, slogans

Bottles, to 9½ inches in height, thrown and slab-built porcelain, raku fired, 2004, by Frank James Fisher, Milford, Michigan.

and extravagant graphics. (I should know; I've created my fair share of mass communication in the form of ads, brochures and packaging over the years.) How could I create an American vessel that reflected our modern society? First, the ceramic vessel should become the packaging and container for an imagined product. Second, the surface should speak the mass-produced language of our society. Finally, 200 years from now, the vessel should act like a time capsule. In other words, it should become an abbreviated snapshot of the moment, rather than a complete explanation of the times.

Commercial printing—actually all printing—duplicates a message. I learned the printing side of advertising and marketing through two decades of press checking the print quality on the marketing materials I created. To build a library of images for my graphics, I accumulated used printing plates from print shops. I searched for newspaper plates, advertising plates, packaging plates, small print blocks and even sets of individual lead type. Old or new, I wanted anything that seemed iconic or symbolized deeper issues.

Once transferred onto the porcelain clay surface, the printing plate impressions became the graphic texture for my new line of American products. Some products are common items like beverages or household items, others are impossible products like war. By selecting specific portions from the printing plates, I could edit the content and create a unified theme for each packaging design. For specific phrases or graphics, printer's lead type was set in blocks and impressed into the clay. To "print color," I turned to raku to give impact to the clay packaging. Raku provides a unique graphic quality that brings out a lively spontaneous feel to the surface. By wiping the glazes on and off, the details of the debossed type and graphics are captured. My artwork moves through familiar ground. My advertising aesthetics are being applied to clay to create my art. But is it really art or is it commercial art? Well, even the label commercial art contains the word art. Yes, I am definitely creating art. And my commercial art colleagues believe it to be the best art the world has ever seen. That sounds like an ad headline—or maybe a testimonial?

Tim Proud
Nomadic Artifacts

by Glen R. Brown

"Black and White Raku Box with Lattice Window," approximately **10 inches in length.**

Like ancient satelites spun from orbit onto a trillion-mile trajectory through space, the raku slab constructions of British ceramist Tim Proud emblematize immeasurable distance, aeonian existence and absolute solitude. Their aura is of the prehistoric artifact, which, for its mere survival across the millennia, commands the reverence of all things immortal. But Proud's pieces are nomadic as well.

Through their allusions to endless journeys with origins and motives in an obscure past, his works condense the effect of the infinite into the concreteness of the handmade object, acquiring a kind of mythical density beyond the physical weight of their materials. The result is an undeniable sense of the spiritual, a distillation of human persistence and energy into pure potential for motion through space and time.

Tim Proud raku firing in Tasmania.

Proud has always associated self-realization with journeying, the process of charting milestones. A native of Durham, England, he attended public school in Scarborough, where a favorite weekend activity was the sport of orienteering. With map and compass in hand, Proud and his classmates traversed the open landscape seeking predetermined landmarks, such as the prehistoric menhirs of standing stones that stud the British isles.

Yellow fields of flowering rape, open moorlands and the vast solitude of the Yorkshire coastline suggested blank planes on which imaginary lines of travel radiated outward from every point. Following them has been Proud's passion: a line projected off a fingertip toward the distant horizon, he observes, may seem as straight as the line penciled between two points on a map, but walking the uneven ground itself yields the multitude of small discoveries that define a life.

Much of Proud's figurative orienteering has led him through academia. After receiving honors in his bachelor of arts degree from Manchester Polytechnic in 1970, Proud completed a yearlong course leading to a postgraduate art teacher's certificate at Leeds University. Fresh from college, he found that the combination of his new job at Ripon Grammar School in Yorkshire and responsibility for a young family left little opportunity for travel. By 1979, however, when he accepted the position of course leader in studio ceramics at the College of Art in Harrogate, Proud was determined to begin following as many imaginary lines as possible. The first of these led south to the Aegean, where he encountered Turkish ceramics, Greek sarcophagi and the inspiration for a series of pieces embodying the concepts of containment and preservation.

The works Proud produced under the influence of ancient Aegean forms were small raku boxes that in his mind took on the character of Turkish houses. "Boxes," he explains, "have a housing value. Soon my boxes became homes for small artifacts."

To emphasize this protective aspect, Proud made pins to hold the lids in place and used matt lusters to give the surfaces the patination of antique cast-iron reliquaries. The unexpected is always a potential consequence of exploration, however, and Proud found that the ritually protective aspect of his boxes could be misinterpreted in favor of more mundane, utilitarian purposes. "People began to stuff things in them," he laughs. "There's nothing worse than finding buttons and paperclips stored in your work."

In order to thwart this temptation, he began sealing his boxes. When that proved too alienating, though, he was compelled to search for other solutions.

As frequently occurs, Proud found that life transitions brought about important changes in his art, realigning its motives and presenting

"Matt Fumed Copper Marker," approximately 15 inches in height, slab built.

"Silver White Marker with Horizon Line," approximately 23 inches in height, raku box.

an array of new questions to be addressed. In 1990, the School of Design at Duncan of Jordanstone College of the University of Dundee was in the process of reassessing its commitment to its ceramics program. When Proud was offered the position of course director in ceramics, he jumped at the chance to move north to Scotland, relishing the opportunity to explore new horizons. As it happened, the move coincided with another major event—the death of Proud's mother.

"These were powerful changes for me," he remembers. "As you get older, you begin to question your orientation and your associations, too. All of a sudden, I was in a new place with a different set of rules."

Within a short period of time, his work began to reflect the influence of his new surroundings. Looking out across the Firth of Forth, it is common to glimpse distant oil rigs—odd, roughly pyramidal forms rising from the flat expanse of salt water—as they are towed in from the North Sea for repair. Combining this singular image with an impression of a starkly geometric church steeple in the nearby fishing village of St. Monans, Proud began to produce eight-sided, diamond-shaped stoppers that project their upper halves from the tops of boxes like pyramids. Set into the heart of the reliquary/house forms, these diamond elements acquire the mystique of crystals or, more fittingly, lodestones. The magnetic heart of these pieces is thus both a source of spiritual attraction and a symbolic orienting device, a mysterious compass that both compels motion and directs it.

Although Proud disavows any adherence to organized religion, he admits an affinity to religious imagery. In his recent works, the four columns supporting the corners of the reliquary forms represent both a relation to family and the apotropaic quality of a childhood prayer: "Matthew, Mark, Luke and John, guard the bed that I lay on."

The immediate visual inspiration for the columns, however, was the concrete stanchions of the Tay Rail Bridge, which support the tons of steel that regularly hurtle across the Firth of Tay south of Dundee. The concepts of power and perpetual motion suggested by a locomotive rushing through mid air on thin steel rails are condensed in Proud's work into the simple configuration of the reliquary with its spiritually charged cargo set upon four sturdy legs whose tapered tips suggest speed and agility.

Some of the developments in his work were prompted by a three-month artist's residency at the University of Tasmania in Launceston in 1995. Like tourists collecting souvenirs, the pieces began to acquire new appendages in reference to the blade-shaped brittle eucalyptus leaves that scatter the Tasmanian hills. These thin, horizontal elements impale the pyramidal forms like splinters of glass hurled by the force of gale winds, reinforcing the concepts of energy and motion al-

"Blue and Red Raku Box on Ball Feet," approximately 11 inches in height, by Tim Proud, Dundee, Scotland.

ready embodied by Proud's works. Perhaps even more influential was the intensity of the Tasmanian light, which set him to thinking about the shadows cast by his pieces upon the ground and each other. The sundial quality of the pyramids was a fitting, if unexpected, revelation that tied the works even more closely to the process of orienting the self in space and time.

Self-orientation was the concern that had initially led Proud to the raku technique, one that he admits does not readily lend itself to the kind of precision he desires. Normally, he produces a series of identical pieces that, despite his use of a template for shaping the slabs, end up possessing unique characteristics. "Usually out of those 10 or 11 pieces, the first one or two are very hesitant, and the last one or two are very tired," he observes. "The ones in the middle are selected as being the strongest because they fulfill all the requirements I place on them: no chips, no cracks, no blemishes."

The risks involved with raku, however, make possible the revelations that Proud most values. "Raku is not just a process," he explains. "It's a spiritual, contemplative, almost Zen-like preparation of materials, an almost fastidiously handling of the contents of the clay. The familiarity of repeating the process moves your consciousness into an unconscious act. Because it's laid down with a sense of structured boundary, the whole process becomes something that is second nature, and the results often surprise me."

Even Proud cannot be sure where his work will lead him next. At the moment, his enthusiasm is divided between research into the use of talc and molochite to strengthen the clay body of his raku pieces, and an exploration of surface treatments that involve stamping impressions into the clay slabs. "As you press something into clay, the clay's got to go somewhere," he notes. "It tends to move around the edges so that when you glaze over the top it produces almost a quilted quality."

If the ripples and puckering bear an analogy to the creases and wrinkles that age impresses into human skin, so much the better. Such marks are the evidence of movement through time. "What I like," Proud says, "is the sequence of events that takes me from one stage to another. I'm an optimistic traveler. I enjoy the journey much more than I do the arrival."

Michael Gustavson
Success Without Compromise

by Jane Reichhold

**"Autumn Shadows,"
31 inches in height,
wheel thrown and
altered.**

Can a potter be a financial success without compromising artistic integrity? Michael Gustavson would be quick to tell you that all it takes is a lot of hard work, many tons of clay and a secret ingredient—focus.

Climbing the few steps to the wide French doors of his white clapboard studio, one can already feel a sense of purpose in the long, two-story building. Rows of large windows follow the sun from east to west as it swings across the Pacific ocean, which crashes at the bottom of cliffs below a dip of sea meadows. Inside, every table and surface is filled with great wet slabs and 3-foot-diameter discs that are drying, waiting to be scraped, or holding their pencil-drawn designs for the final application of glazes. Great vessels stand on tables around the two small electric wheels. These vessels, rising up to 36 inches in height, seem to be giant soap bubbles that twist and stretch beyond all reason. Even in their raw, unglazed state, the strength and power of their unbelievable forms captivate the attention of even the most casual observer.

Gustavson, whose wide, muscle-bound shoulders reflect the abundance of his pots, is quick to share his secrets because he views his knowledge as a gift and he knows each person can only make their own sculpture. He stretches the clay into these shapes as manifestations of his own energy in relation to the spiritual relationship he has with the world.

For the person who discovers Gustavson's work in one of over a dozen galleries sprinkled across the United States, it is usually the surface design that is most immediately compelling. Rising up from a fire-blackened background, the controlled circles, ovoids, triangles and organic shapes in bright reds, oranges, greens, deep blues and purples shift and move across the surface. Among these colors are the shaded lusters and metallics of raku reduction, and the lumpy lava crusts that crack open to reveal even more sub-

"Chromatic Afternoon,"
74 inches in width,
slab built.

tle undertones. Here it is revealed that Gustavson thinks of himself as a painter, but one who makes his canvas out of clay.

Nothing Gustavson does is off-hand or lacking in focus. He knows production can deaden one's joy of exploring, so he takes new steps and makes changes in the smallest increments. For instance, he began to explore a more painterly approach with brushed edges around bright yellows, oranges and reds.

Gustavson has an M.F.A. from San Jose State College. However, he feels schools often spend more time pushing students to "find their individual voice" and not enough time educating them on the necessity of focusing on a goal or teaching them marketing skills so they can earn a living in the profession that they went to school to learn. He admits there is a balancing act between what people want to buy and what an artist wants to make. An even greater achievement is to have found success, and continue to evolve and develop new ideas. He is always learning from the reality of the markets. Galleries will often put his vessels in their windows because

"Looking Forward,"
68 inches in width,
slab built.

they will stop the passers by in their tracks long enough to get them to come in the door. And yet, the wall pieces outsell the vessels two to one—people have more wall space to cover with art than they have places to properly display sculpture.

Both of Gustavson's children work with their father in all phases, from production to the delivery of items to galleries to the setting up of shows. Gustavson unobtrusively teaches his kids, even at the openings of other shows. He will first ask, "Have you looked at everything? Okay, which is the piece that best exemplifies the theme of the show?" Then they walk to each person's choice to look at it and regard his or her opinion. Finally, Gustavson opines on his choice and leaves it up to each to agree or disagree with him. Sometimes the question varies to "Which is the best piece in this show?" or, "Which piece is getting the most attention?" or, "Which work do you think will sell first?" Gustavson believes in the old-world method of an education, where sons and daughters are taught their parents' skills and then encouraged to find their own way.

"Drama," 29 inches in height, wheel thrown and altered, by Michael Gustavson, Gualala, California.

Building and Firing Large Raku Vessels

To begin a vessel, Gustavson throws a 15–50-pound gumdrop-shaped wad of Soldate clay into a cylinder and then lets it spin on the wheel overnight to dry and to allow the clay particles to adjust to the new shape. Then, with rubber kidneys of various sizes and hardness, he begins from the inside, stroke by stroke, to ease and tease the walls to bow outward. The old adage that the shape of a vessel comes from the inside is never more true than in the way Gustavson creates these sculptural forms. This slow process continues until the vessel walls are perfectly thin and sinuous. Sometimes the neck is completely closed so the organic shape seems like an enlarged, growing amoebic life form. He explains that no matter how huge the vessel and how often people are told never to pick one up by the lip, someone will—and he is prepared for them. He adds a flattened coil to the under-side of the opening for strength. Sometimes this edge is rounded and smoothed so the walls appear quite thick. Other times, he leaves the reinforcing collar to imitate the neck of a t-shirt, so the vessel almost resembles decorative clothing that dances with a ghostly being inside. The vessels are scraped as smooth on the outside as they are on the inside and are then left to dry.

Now comes the hardest part of all: lifting the large greenware objects down into the 40-inch top-loading kiln. As he makes the final arrangement, leaning far into the kiln, he either hooks his feet under a nearby table top or has an assistant hold his legs to keep from toppling in on his pots.

He bisque fires the pieces to cone 06 in one of his two electric kilns. He uses the other one for reducing glazes with pine needles. No, this is not a recommended procedure, but he does it any-how—and it works. After the load has reached maturity, he allows it to cool to below 1000°F. He then opens the lid and throws in pine needles. The elements in this kiln do not seem to wear out any faster than those in his other kiln. He also has a gas raku kiln outdoors where he picks up the glowing slabs to place them in reduction bins.

As fascinating as Gustavson's vessels are, one cannot help noticing that far more space in the studio is given to the 24–38-inch slabs of clay. When they are laid out on the floor, covering one end of the building, they seem to be islands of clay floating over the cement floor or giant, pale lily pads on a pond of white water. Automatically, one looks around for an immense slab roller and finds none. Gustavson rolls each of these 1-inch-thick slabs out by hand (his favorite technique) in order to ease and stretch the lump of clay into perfect flatness. He carefully chips around the perimeter of the nearly-dry slab to get an irregular, organic edge. This technique is a reminder of the shards of a broken, glazed pot that first gave him the idea to make these works.

So precise is Gustavson that he actually draws a pattern to determine the proper way to hang his multipart wall works. He lays the sections on heavy brown paper, moving them around until he is completely satisfied with the way the design flows from one to another and the negative spaces between have gained their own importance. Then he draws the outline of the pieces, making holes in the paper where the screws will go into the wall so the hangers fit perfectly.

Barbara Harnack
Archetypal Tribe

by Hollis Walker

The view from the hilltop home and studio of Barbara Harnack and her husband, Michael Lancaster, just south of Santa Fe, New Mexico, is vast and colorful. Perpetually clear blue skies and evergreen-studded mountains stretch into the horizon. Below, the earth is incised by dusty arroyos and winding dirt roads, interrupted here and there by both modest and magnificent adobe homes, the occasional horse corral, the remains of a miner's shack.

Before moving to New Mexico in 1987, Harnack made functional stoneware in upstate New York. She began to experiment with figurative ceramics, and once ensconced in the light and landscape of New Mexico, she felt the need to create larger pieces in brighter colors, and

Barbara Harnack feeds a reduction barrel with straw outside of her adobe home and studio. During Harnack's raku process, sculptures are rotated and barrels are refueled two to three times. Some barrels are left open to reoxidize to finish and control carbonization. Photo by S.B. Khalsa.

to explore, in clay, her first love of drawing.

Since moving, she has embraced raku as her firing process, and turned entirely to drawing, sculpting and painting the figure in clay. Her colorful, upright, slab-built works stand witness to her intuitive drive to follow the figure: Male and female, human and animal, they evoke archetypes both mysterious and benevolent, unnamable but nonetheless recognizable.

The individuals in Harnack's mental "tribe" appear and reappear in her sculptures, and the process of making them, though requiring consummate technical skill, is also an intuitive one. She doesn't sketch her figures in advance; instead, she lets the clay speak to her of what it should become.

Harnack works from large slabs of commercial clay laid flat on a table. She cuts out a figure—usually head and torso—determining in the process its sex, size and shape. She sometimes rips the edges of the clay to create rough edges. Lifting the slab figure—usually between two and three feet tall—she gently shapes it into a semicircle so that it will stand alone, briefly allowing it to rest and stabilize. Using her hands, she may add remnants of the clay slab like patches and otherwise manipulate the clay to create a subtle three-dimensional surface, adding a nose, chin, breasts or arms. Using a pin tool, comb and a brush cleaner as scratching tools, she draws freehand on and into the sur-

face, both for figurative detail, such as eyes, and for texture and depth. Raw spots and broken edges are treated as naturally occurring phenomena; she doesn't try to repair or perfect them. When she is satisfied with the essential features of her figure, Harnack bisques the piece in an electric kiln.

After the initial firing, the artist cleans the figure's surface of any irregularities and glazes it, again using a spontaneous process to choose colors and where to apply them, as well as what areas to leave bare so they will carbonize and turn black during the firing sequence. Incorporating nearly forty colors into her glaze palette, Harnack applies color like a wash, in several thin layers, sometimes adding glaze, then scrubbing it away, then adding more. She eschews metal glazes, as she finds those without metal have a more painterly feel.

When she's satisfied with the glazing, she and Lancaster fire the pieces in their raku kiln. During the smoking, Harnack and Lancaster may add more straw or move the pieces around in the barrels to facilitate the process. "The smoking element is what I consider really critical," Harnack explains. "It distinguishes the expression of each artwork. It gives it soul, quite frankly."

Firing fifteen to twenty times a year, the couple has developed a keen sense of what works. Still, Harnack routinely reglazes and refires her figures, sometimes three times, before she is satisfied with

Pro-Active Raku Firing

by Barbara Harnack with Michael Lancaster

We began raku firing in 1977 at The Malden Bridge School of Art. This was one of several week-long workshops we led with guest teachers. Our technique was pretty standard: fire until red hot, remove ware from kiln (while experiencing searing pain) and toss into a barrel of newspaper/sawdust/pine needles as quickly as possible. Cover it up. Ten minutes later, open the barrel and reveal the results. Some were great, while others were tepid, boring or over reduced.

After many years of experimentation, the one part of raku firing that has changed for us the most is the reduction or smoking. Some of our ideas followed the observation of what happens to a long fire in a fireplace after it cools. There, we found a clean area where the carbon had re-oxidized from red heat, a color layer where the smoke had entered the slight porosity of the bricks during the transition from red heat to no red heat, and a sooty area where there was smoke but no red heat. The important "zone" (the middle area) is between 1200–900°F. All raku ware and its intended result will be up to the ceramist to determine. It does not matter whether or not one is working with fuming, metallic glazes or finishes, clear glazes and underglaze colors, or a matt or burnished raw clay. What is most important is that as an artist, one must make a conscious decision to interact with what happens in those final smoking or fuming stages. There are a number of personal decisions to make: protective gear for hands and body, respiratory protection, factors of wind and fire hazards. In the end we always treat the smoke as if it's a paint or glaze and we interact with it.

"Way Round," 30½ inches in height, slab built, with underglazes, 2006, by Barbara Harnack, Cerillos, New Mexico.

the way they look and feel, how the raku crazing interacts with her drawing marks and the painted areas. Once fired, the figures have a human sensibility they didn't have as greenware shapes.

In her early years in New Mexico, Harnack was exposed for the first time to the simple, hand-carved wooden saints (santos) of the Spanish Colonial folk art tradition. Made as devotional items and often displayed in churches and homes, the figures had historically been dressed in fabric clothing and sometimes had decorative elements. But the antique santos Harnack saw typically had lost their clothing, crowns

"Farm State," 26 inches in height, slab built, with underglazes, 2006.

ceramic figures, once fired, evoke the same response: their "scars," intentional and otherwise, imbue them with humanity and compassion. Harnack says she hopes their owners feel them as benevolent, empathetic presences in their lives. Often, patrons buy two or more figures and display them together, in relationship. That pleases Harnack, who, after all, sees them as part of a "family" of sorts.

Some of the characters she creates appear and reappear in slightly different forms. "I have an elderly woman who keeps showing up, who's very kindly; maybe she's an unconscious tribute to Madam Sorrell," Harnack muses.

In addition to her large figurative works, Harnack also makes smaller, similar pieces—busts, in effect—and draws and paints her unique faces on clay vases Lancaster throws.

While the engineering process of making the larger figures is a challenge, Harnack remains gratified by her creative method. "Drawing in the raku is a wonderful discipline for me, because it's all the things I delight in: the drawing, the immediacy and the richness that's possible with both of the disciplines incorporated with each other. Glazing and firing offer more layers for expressing myself." And, though she has learned to control the formation of the figures and their ornamentation, the last step always holds a promise to surprise. "That's the real delight of the process—not knowing the outcome until after the firing."

or other accessories over the years; sometimes a limb had fallen off, the wood had discolored or split, or other calamities had befallen them. To the artist, the wooden dolls revealed more in their nakedness and damaged condition than if they had been pristine; they embodied the emotional suffering all humans suffer as a natural consequence of living. Her

Gone Fishing
Firing the Catch

by Diana Pittis

From top to bottom: Queen Triggerfish, 14½ inches in length, slab-built Laguna LB Blend/Soldate 60 mixture, with stains, oxides and glazes, fired to cone 05, with post-firing reduction.

I'd been throwing for thirty years and my arms were protesting. In the process of eliminating throwing from my work, I began making slab-molded pieces. To transition from functional pottery to sculptural forms, I produced a series of tall, abstract "totem" pieces. It didn't take long to realize that there was a limited market for these works in Appalachia. I needed to find a sculptural form everyone could relate to. I made my first fish in 2002.

My first two fish were anatomically incorrect, but they had character, spunk and, more importantly, sold quickly. I didn't have a clue what a fish really looked like, so I visited the fish section of a local grocery store and had a good look. Then a friend gave me two books, which I understand to be the fisherman's "bibles" along the Atlantic coast, especially around Florida. Armed with these photographs, I began making fish that looked like actual fish. Again, these sold quite readily. So now I could focus on the technical issues.

The Forming Process

First, I make a paper template and cut out two slabs. I wrap the edges of the slabs with plastic to keep them from drying. Next, I drape them on cardboard cylinders of varying diameters to give some dimension to the fish body. When dry enough, I add slip on the edges and assemble the slabs. I then cut a small hole in the bottom of the fish where a custom-made iron stand will ultimately go. I blow into this hole and the fish puffs out. It usually ruptures somewhere along the seam so I just plug up that seam opening and have another go. At this point, I place the rough fish on a stand that I designed.

The sculpting stand is an iron tube that fits inside the bottom of the fish. It has an oval collar and sits on a rod mounted to the base. The collar supports the fish and swivels. This allows me to work on the entire fish with the small exception of the collar-supported area.

The fish are fired in bisqued fired cradles and specially-designed tongs are used to easily remove them from the kiln for post-firing reduction.

Firing Cradle

For raku firing, I came up with the idea of making a "cradle" to hold the fish so I could glaze them all over. I throw a bottomless cylinder about 5 inches tall, with a wide flange on the exterior about 1 inch from the rim. I then squeeze this into an oval and cut a groove in both ends. One groove holds the head of the fish, and the other holds the rear. The flange provides the necessary surface area to grasp and lift the cradle quickly without touching the fish. The fish only touches the cradle at two tiny spots, and I dab a bit of alumina hydrate there. The only problem that I have encountered is that cradles break after about three firings.

Firing Tongs

I also had to specially design and manufacture iron tongs that could lift the cradles that hold the fish. These tongs allow for the necessary leverage and speed to unload the kiln rapidly, and they work terrifically. The cradle and tongs allow me to make larger fish. The largest I've made so far is 26 inches long.

Glazes

I knew that if I was trying sculpturally to make a fish that had the proportions of a real fish, I should also try to stay somewhat true to their actual colors. I sprayed muriatic acid on Alligator Matt glazed fish during the cooling process. I also applied a clear glaze on portions of the glaze to break up the very matt look. I currently use only two glazes: Alligator Matt White and a White Crackle glaze. I rub stains on the bisqued fish to highlight the scales, spray one of the two glazes, spray stains and oxides, then perhaps spray one of the two glazes again.

Firing

I fire to cone 05, and I pre-bisque my cone packs for raku so that they don't blow up in the early part of the firing. I use a raku kiln that fires up like a rocket. The first firing takes about an hour and fifteen minutes; thereafter, about forty minutes. I have to let it cool down at least twenty minutes before reloading.

I have a few 55-gallon steel drums and miscellaneous metal cans, but none were suitable for unloading a 26-inch-long fish and the cradle, which, together, are pretty heavy. I came up with the idea of reducing in a big cardboard box. I get big boxes from wherever I can find them (I'm a box aficionado and have been known to follow store clerks who are about to cut up an ideal box). Using long boxes, I cut three sides of the top to make a "flap-lidded" cardboard box. For the necessary speed required for proper reduction, the fish must be removed and enclosed within the box very quickly. This requires two people. As I remove a cradled fish from the kiln and place it into the box, an assistant holds back the lid, then shuts it and places a board on top for weight. These boxes are pre-packed with an assortment of shredded paper, sawdust, dried grass and other combustible material. They burn down completely and are quite the pyromaniac's dream.

Pittis describes her post-firing reduction method as "a pyromaniac's dream." Rather than using unwieldy 55-gallon metal drums, she uses large cardboard boxes prepacked with shredded paper, sawdust, dried grass and other combustible materials.

83

Striped Bass, 16 inches in length, slab-built Laguna LB Blend/Soldate 60 mixture, with stains, oxides and glazes, fired to cone 05, with post-firing reduction; by Diana Pittis, Daniels, West Virginia.

Finishing Touches

The final step in completing these fish is to attach the stand. I turn them upside down in a foam-padded holder, stuff rags into the bottom opening of the fish to block the mouth then pour a liquid mix of concrete into the opening at the bottom of the fish with a funnel. I then position the iron stand and wire into place so that the fish will sit at the proper angle. The mounted fish range in length from 11 to 26 inches and weigh anywhere from 8 to 16 pounds—clay, concrete and iron combined. The final step for each fish is to be signed on the bottom.

Recipes

Raku White Crackle
Cone 05
Gerstley Borate	80 %
Nepheline Syenite	20
	100 %

Alligator Matt White
Cone 05
Bone Ash	29 %
Gerstley Borate	57
Nepheline Syenite	14
	100 %

A Sense of Timelessness

by Jimmy Clark

"Globe Pot,"
14 inches in height,
pinched, brushed
with terra sigillata,
pit fired, partially
stripped, sanded
and sealed, by
Jimmy Clark.

Pinching is an ancient hand-building technique that allows the maker to interact directly with the clay. In my work, the consistency of the material, its reactions to atmospheric conditions and my own mood or subconscious are given free rein to affect the final form. The desired result is a sense of timelessness—a sense that the pot has had a long life of its own, independent of its creator. Ultimately, I like to think of myself as but one of three integral elements that share equal responsibility for the work's creation: artist, material, and fire.

My vessels are freely formed while resting on my lap or in sling molds made by loosely spanning a bucket or other round container with a towel. I do have several start-up techniques that direct the pot toward a particular shape (i.e., oval, tall, open or closed), but often I find the clay

"Storage Jar with Spirit Hole," 12½ inches in height, pinched from a single ball of clay, brushed with terra sigillata, and pit fired in sawdust.

"Bowl," 12 inches in height, pinched, brushed with terra sigillata, pit fired, partially stripped, sanded and sealed, then accented with inlaid copper.

"Bowl with Copper Patch," 9½ inches in height, pinched, brushed with terra sigillata, broken, pit fired and reassembled.

leading in a totally different direction, and have learned that following the clay is vastly preferable to struggling with it.

Despite a preoccupation with larger forms in recent years, I usually restrict myself to pinching the piece out of a single ball of clay. At one time, I explored the size limitations of this process and pinched out an entire 25-pound bag of prepared clay, but for the most part my larger forms begin as 10- to 15-pound balls.

I like to think of these pots as asymmetrical balloons blown up to the brink of bursting. The walls of the resulting forms are often extremely thin and fragile. Sometimes, this fragility leads to breakage of one kind or another, but in recent years I have begun to incorporate these occurrences as yet another event contributing to the vessel's history and ultimate appearance.

The most common forms of breakage are what I refer to as "spirit holes," inspired by the spirit bowls of the ancient Mimbres of the Southwest. I have come to appreciate these small breakthroughs, which often

**"Bottomless Pot with Brass Stand,"
10½ inches in height, pinched,
rubbed with crocus martis, burnished
and pit fired, by Jimmy Clark.**

occur during burnishing, and their seemingly predestined placement as enhancements to the form. Other more dramatic mishaps, which may occur during firing or through random accidents, may be addressed by inserting copper patches and decorating with metallic paint.

Concluding this intuitive approach is my preferred firing method—pit firing—which blackens the surfaces in totally unpredictable and uncontrollable ways. To achieve deep blacks, I used to purposely retard the firings, allowing very little air into the kiln and burning the finest sawdust I could find. One particularly slow-burning firing retained glimmering ashes eleven days after ignition. More recently, however, I have become fascinated with the flashings and color variations that come with faster firings done with coarser sawdust and increased air flow.

The larger scale of my recent work has led me to experimenting with terra sigillata. Applications to bisqueware resulted in a glorious "mistake," where most of the sigillata peeled off like bad paint in the pit fire. After the balance was scraped off, a singularly rich and varied pattern (resembling spider webs intertwined with cartography) remained.

In addition to the peeled-terra-sigillata technique, I have begun to subject the pots to multiple firings. I find that these more varied surfaces increase the sense of "history" for each vessel.

David Greenbaum
Flowing with Balance and Harmony

by Mary Ann DeMuth

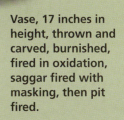

After many years, David Greenbaum's claywork has come full circle. "As potters, we have many different directions we can pursue," he says. "I believe our work in clay is reflective, as it should be, of our personal lives—our spiritual journey. After exploring so many avenues, I returned to the comfort of the pots I began with. I found that my technique flowed easily; it was not forced. As a result, I'm making the best pots of my life and I've never known more joy working with clay."

Such joy often eluded Greenbaum during the course of his career, primarily because of his manic drive to constantly innovate, to leave past creations behind in favor of the elusive cutting edge. However, he has always been drawn to the process of making pots. "The organic quality of the process is so direct. I adore sticking my hands in the mud and shaping it. It's that grittiness that rang true for me from the start."

Greenbaum was a 21-year-old Ithaca College student with no art background when he met a potter who had a workshop in the dorm basement. At first, he was attracted to the potter's lifestyle, but once he had learned the basics, he couldn't stop making pots. He apprenticed for a year with Rhode Island potter Dwight Graves, then ventured out on his own, establishing a pottery in Virginia. "Initially, I was inspired by Southwestern pottery. It appealed to me aesthetically, as did much of the Native American culture," he explains. "I found the simplicity of the primitive techniques

Vase, 17 inches in height, thrown and carved, burnished, fired in oxidation, saggar fired with masking, then pit fired.

Intricate carving has become an enjoyable meditation for Greenbaum.

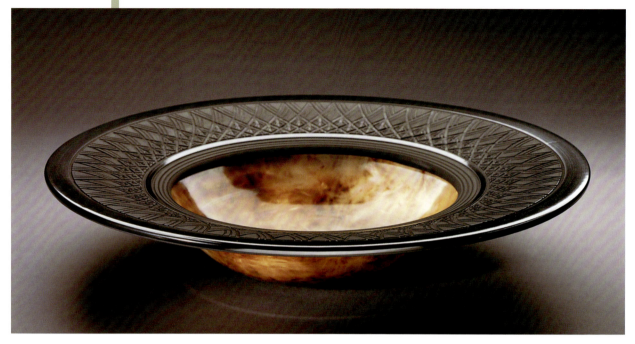

Wide-rimmed bowl, 23 inches in diameter, thrown and carved, burnished on the wheel, saggar fired with masking, then pit fired in grasses and pine needles.

and the elegance of the classic forms appealing."

From Virginia, Greenbaum moved to Florida. Though he had arrived at a style of pottery that satisfied him and appealed to buyers, he began to think he also had to move on artistically. He experimented with a wide array of stylistic variations, everything from 400-pound soda-fired vessels to kitchenware. Over the years, he also built several houses and studios as he searched for the perfect environment in which to live and work.

After more than two decades of full-time potting, Greenbaum grew frustrated with his ever-present obsession to innovate. He completely abandoned clay and went into the canoe and kayak business for a few years. He found a measure of contentment on the beautiful Santa Fe

River, but he also found he missed his pots. Eventually, he sold the canoe business and returned to pottery.

"I came back to pottery with a lot of questions about my motivation," he remembers. "I spun my wheels because I did not have the confidence to go with my heart. I was holding onto my old feeling that I had to innovate constantly—what I made had to be new to be valid. As I struggled with all of this, I had this flash of realization that it's okay to make pots that simply flow out of me, pots that are not forced."

Greenbaum attributes his arrival at this awareness to a number of factors, including growing older. "Aging is simply the greatest gift of life," he says. "With experience comes awareness, and with awareness come growth and wisdom. There is

Platter, 32 inches in diameter, wheel thrown, carved and burnished, then saggar fired, by David Greenbaum.

no other way to acquire them than by living."

When Greenbaum throws, he is focused on the design and perfection of the form. He prefers the classic shapes produced by potters for thousands of years. "These forms have withstood the test of time," he says. "There's a reason they have endured so long. A pure form is balanced and harmonious. When I throw a pot, I concentrate on finding its harmony. When it clicks, there is a certain rightness and an inarguable truth and unity."

Just as he strives for perfection of form, he also spends a great deal of time perfecting his carving and burnishing methods. His production is limited, so each pot receives a lot of attention. He uses handmade tools for carving—usually looped guitar strings that leave precise incisions. When he begins to carve, he relies only on experience to create perfectly spaced, repeating patterns.

Greenbaum prefers to burnish rather than glaze his pots, even though it is more time consuming. Using a polished stone, he burnishes the pots on the wheel. First, he moistens the bone-dry pot with water, and burnishes it until the surface is smooth. Next, he applies a thin coating of olive oil, and repeats the process. The wheel's rotation helps to eliminate burnishing marks.

If the pot's surface is to be ivory, Greenbaum applies terra sigillata before burnishing, and fires it in oxidation. For his black pots, he follows the oxidation firing with a saggar firing. His newest pots feature two tones: black and the warm honey color of burl wood. For these, he masks the portions he doesn't want affected by the carbon in the saggar firing. Then, he removes the mask and does a third firing in an open pit where burning pine needles and grasses impart the wood-like coloration.

He divides his time between carving days and throwing days, while keeping the kilns humming. "When I was a younger guy, it took a lot of discipline for me to sit and carve for eight hours," he remembers. "Now, I look forward to the meditative unfolding of the designs. It's not forced labor at all."

Greenbaum's return to clay was accompanied by a change in the way he sold his pots. Preferring the retail experience to wholesale, he now sells primarily at art fairs, along with a handful of galleries. "Part of my joy is the retail experience," he says. "It's defined and concrete, and it has an immediacy and directness that appeal to me. I get great satisfaction from interacting with people who love my pots."

The booth he uses at six to eight art fairs each year has a quiet presence and features a small, select inventory. He believes potential customers are attracted by the serenity of his presentation.

Gallery owners who show his work tend to be those with whom he has had a close relationship over the years. "It's as much about the interpersonal contact as it is the business relationship. I really like these people, and they present my work well," Greenbaum says.

The results of his redefined direction and sales approach have been "all the business I can deal with at the moment. As the world becomes more digital, I believe handmade items will retain their special, near-sacred place for all of us," he predicts. "While online shopping abounds, I think craft fairs are destined for a long and prosperous future. People yearn to experience art firsthand— to see it and hold it. The retail art market is wonderful for that, and it's a really fun event. As long as the work has your spirit behind it, there will always be a market for it."

Anasazi Pottery
Making Black-on-White Ware

by Jeff Lawrence

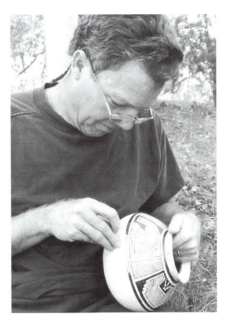

Colorado artist Clint Swink duplicates Anasazi pottery techniques.

Ancient clay artifacts speak to potters of today with a voice that cannot be ignored. To faithfully replicate these artifacts is to answer that voice—to converse with those makers from times past. Naturally, the worthier the artifacts, the more satisfying the achievement.

The Anasazi culture occupied the Four Corners area of the southwestern United States for 14 centuries; the Mesa Verdeans abandoned the area around A.D. 1300. They left behind a rich ceramics legacy, both corrugated culinary ware and the more famous black-on-white pottery, but few production clues.

Cliff Swink, a Colorado artist, became interested in the Anasazi pottery of Mesa Verde many years ago. Primarily a landscape painter, he began sharpening the focus of his work to smaller scenes, often incorporating the potsherds ubiquitous near his home. In search of better models, he attempted first to make pots with commercially prepared materials, but the results were unsatisfactory. He soon realized that

the look he wanted could only be achieved by following in the original makers' footsteps—the authentic process.

There are two distinct issues that replicators must address, and both must be consistent with the archaeological record. First, the materials, techniques and design must have been available prehistorically. Second, the firing process must produce comparable ware and kiln residue.

Swink addressed these issues by firing an actual Anasazi trench kiln located 25 miles northwest of Cortez, Colorado. The kiln had been jointly excavated by a three-man archaeological team led by Joel Brisbin, a Mesa Verde National Park archaeologist, and a three-potter team led by Swink.

Shaping and Decorating

Swink insists on authenticity, using only tools he makes and/or gathers from the land. His construction sequence is: build, smooth, form and finish; followed by slipping, burnishing and painting.

Building involves straightforward handbuilding techniques. First, a flat "pancake" base is made by flinging a wad of clay sideways against a flat surface, turning and flinging it again until it reaches the correct thickness. A functional advantage of this method is that it compresses the clay particles.

Next, a circular base of the appropriate size is cut from the pancake with a sliver of wood. For a bowl, the base is pressed into a shallow potsherd called a *puki*, which keeps the bottom curved while the sides are added.

A coil or "snake" of clay is then rolled between the hands. Mugs usually require only a single coil to build the wall. After a wipe of water on both base and coil, the two pieces are pinched together and the seam carefully smoothed.

The remainder of the shaping involves pinching and scraping, continuing until the shape is satisfactory. Pieces of dried gourds make scrapers that soften with use.

When the vessels are nearly leather hard, wide yucca-leaf brushes are used to apply a coating of slip made from a fine white montmorillonite. This coating is left to dry overnight and part of the next day before burnishing it with smooth stones.

If the slip is not dry enough, the burnishing stone scrapes off large flakes. Even if the coating remains intact, burnishing too-wet slip is futile because the sheen disappears as the slip dries. When almost dry, though, it burnishes to an almost mirrorlike sheen, but if bumps and pits have not been carefully smoothed and filled, the fine slip coating does very little to hide them.

After they are burnished, the pots are ready to be painted, using brushes made from narrow yucca leaves. Softened for weeks in water, the yucca flesh is easily scraped away to leave behind a natural fiber brush.

Painting

After the effort of preparing the surface, the first brushstroke can be positively frightening. Fortunately, Swink insists that workshop participants study and practice the Anasazi designs in advance. Compositions are sketched on paper, then with a soft pencil on the pot itself. This approach produces remarkable results from first-timers.

The "paint" is from an indigenous plant, Rocky Mountain beeplant (cleome serrulata), which Swink boils to reduce to a sticky, aromatic, semisolid that works quite effectively with yucca brushes. This is particularly noticeable when painting multiple fine lines. With even the best contemporary brushes, line thickness varies with brush pressure, and each recharge of the brush leaves some evidence of the interrupted stroke. The yucca brushes gener-

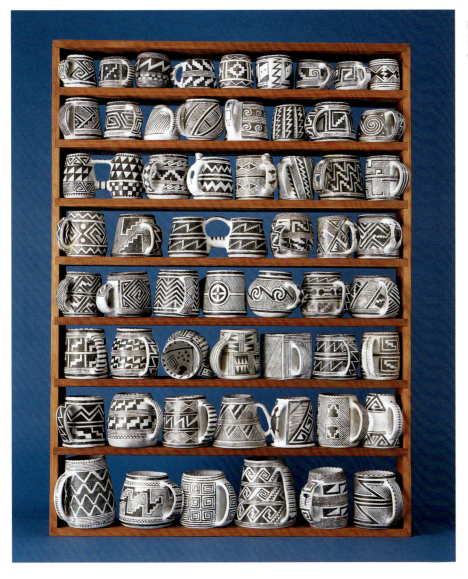

Replicas of actual
Mesa Verde black-
on-white mugs.

ate fine lines with ease. In addition, the wet paint on the pot exhibits an electrostatic attraction for the paint on the brush. Pragmatically, this means that a seamless continuation of a fine line is much easier, since the brush quite literally jumps back into place, leaving no interruption in the line. The emotional conclusion is more animate: "The pots want to be painted."

The sophistication of Anasazi designs deserves mention, even if it is somewhat superficial here. On the whole, these designs strike a pregnant balance between black paint and white ware. Like an optical illusion, the tension of uncertainty is delightful: which is the design and which is the background?

Although the designs appear rigidly geometrical, they are not what

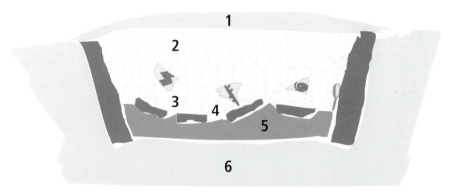

The "Camp Kiln" excavation produced a ladle in the attitude shown (against the wall on the right); it had apparently been overlooked when the kiln was unloaded. From top to bottom, the excavators found 1) post-abandonment fill; 2) redeposited soil; 3) a mixture of charcoal, dirt and shards; 4) rock shelving; 5) dense carbonaceous material; and 6) undisturbed soil or bedrock.

they seem. Virtually all contain some "violation" of the pattern, an area where the predictable element is subtly altered. These cunning visual surprises give each piece its individuality, inviting the viewer into a riddle game with the potter.

Firing

Swink's firing regimen is the product of archaeological study and hundreds of firings, and represents a huge breakthrough to the past. By working with archaeologist Joel Brisbin, excavator of nine trench kilns in Mesa Verde National Park, he has had the opportunity to review kiln stratigraphy (depositional layering of firing residue). Trench kilns are essentially rectangular boxes dug into soil or bedrock, and the walls lined with slabs of rock.

The 35 kilns excavated to date vary little from an average of about 4 feet wide and approximately 14 inches deep. Swink translates this into a universal human scale as "two arm-lengths wide."

All the kilns were situated perpendicular to secondary drainage, a placement that takes advantage of steady, predictable air movement. Then, as now, ample draft was necessary for making temperature.

Typical trench kiln stratigraphy reveals a bottom of dense carbonaceous material often containing chunks of unburnt fuel, followed by a loose pavement of flat rocks. Atop these "shelves" is a tumbled mixture of soil, charcoal and shards. The final layer consists of relatively clean soil.

Analysis of the unburnt fuel has shown that the Anasazi used pinyon pine and juniper; both produce blocky, long-burning coals, which allow enough airflow between them to achieve higher temperatures than with faster-burning types of wood.

Suggestive clues about the oxygen content of the firing atmosphere are also provided by the artifacts. Broken Anasazi ware shows a black reduced core surrounded by a thin white layer. It is clear, then, that a reduction atmosphere was required as part of the firing. At the same time, however, a period of oxidation was necessary to make the surface white. Through his experimentation, Swink has found that this oxidation can be overdone; too much results in yellow and red designs on ware that is more buff than white.

Given these findings, Swink developed the following four-step firing sequence, which produces stratigraphy and ware consistent with the record:

1. A primary fire generates the carbonaceous residue of the lowest layer, dries the kiln and creates a heat source for later stages.

2. The setting involves placing a horizontal layer of stone shelving, thoroughly dried pottery and firing shards.

3. A secondary firing produces the large amount of charcoal found above the shelving and generates most of the firing heat.

4. The smothering phase quenches the fire and creates an oxygen-free cooling environment.

These firings reach temperatures ranging from 1472°F to 1652°F, maintained typically for 30 to 45 minutes.

Primary fire; prevailing winds are from downhill

Setting

Secondary fire

Smothering with dirt (mounded for rain runoff); any vents that form as fuel collapses must be covered.

At our Camp Kiln firing, Swink first burned enough coarse fuel to create an even bed of coals at least 4 inches deep, filling the length of the 6-foot kiln. Atop this primary fuel, stone shelves were laid, leaving up to 3-inch gaps between. After the shelving heated up, the pots were carefully set on the shelving and the spaces between the pots covered with large shards, which both protect the ware from damage and allow air circulation through to the primary fuel bed, reigniting it for a later temperature increase.

En route to developing these techniques, Swink helped the archaeologists understand the role of these firing shards, accounting for the numerous otherwise baffling shards, which had clearly been fired multiple times after being broken. Many shards found near kilns can now be seen simply as tools left behind.

The pots warmed up gradually, drying thoroughly as the paint burned into their surfaces. Several pots not thoroughly dried were split by steam, but the majority came through this stage intact.

When the shards were hot enough to sizzle when touched with a wet finger, the secondary fuel was laid. This consisted of two relatively massive "spanners" laid across the kiln's width. The spanners supported the bulk of the secondary fuel, which was ignited on top. While the secondary fuel burned, it generated radiant heat, which raised the kiln temperature at the relatively slow rate of 68°F per minute.

The pace is vital. If too much fuel burns too quickly, it not only fractures the pots, but makes the secondary fuel collapse and actually insulates the pots with ash and coals. The result of this sequence is dark underfired ware. When burning efficiently and slowly, the secondary fuel distributes heat throughout the setting.

While the flames are roaring (and they do roar), a reduction atmosphere prevails in the setting because the fuel is greedy for available oxygen. During this time, the ware is completely black—blackened not only from the fire but from within as the carbonaceous material in the clay burns.

When the flames ebb, oxygen becomes more plentiful and limited oxidation begins, turning the slip white at peak temperature. It is at this point that the fire must be smothered with soil. If it cools and overoxidizes, white and black change to orange and buff. It is crucial when smothering to watch for venting to the outside as the fuel collapses—a vent will feed oxygen to the fire, letting it smolder for days and overoxidizing the pots.

A day later, the soil was removed by hand and the ware extracted. This stage of the firing can only be conducted by hand, as digging tools would damage the ware. Consequently, the best approach is

Trench-kiln-fired Anasazi-style ware before cleanup.

for one pair of hands to sift through the shards, dirt, charcoal and rocks to uncover the pots.

Slowly, 700 years after its last use, the kiln revealed the fruits of our workshop labor: perfect replicas of Mesa Verde black-on-white pottery. Even the blemishes inevitable in open firings of this type were themselves replicas of Anasazi firing flaws. Fortunately, these pots could easily be refired later for a more pleasing result. The retrieval of the ware produced exactly the mixed layer of soil, shards and charcoal found at the excavated kilns.

In effect, knowledge reclaimed through archaeological dialogue with ancient potters has formed a clay bridge from the past to wider possibilities in contemporary ceramics.

Testing in the Pit

by Sumi von Dassow

Pit loaded with pots and ready to fire as soon as the wood is put in on top of the pots. Underneath the pots is a layer of sawdust with salt, Miracle-Gro and copper sulfate mixed in. The test pots are scattered throughout the pit, many on their sides to protect them from ash from above.

No lime green! I don't want any lime green on my pots!... I want only a little bit of black. How can I get lots of that peach color? What will copper wire do if I put it on my pot? What will banana peels do? What will coffee grounds do?

Participants in a pit firing excitedly place their orders as I load up a pit for firing. Avoiding lime green is easy—just don't put the pot near copper wire. Avoiding black isn't too hard if I just keep the pot out of the wood shavings at the bottom of the pit, but often the pots that don't get much black on them also don't get a lot of other color on them either. As for the peach color, well, we all hope for that and we'll do our best.

What to Test

The "what will this or that do" questions will be answered (I hope) by a series of test pots I'm putting in the pit. I've made 20 or so bowls with small pots that fit inside, and each one is filled with a different material or combination of materials. Into most I've placed a handful of wood shavings with a tablespoon or so of some chemical mixed in, then nestled the small pot into the shavings. Here's what I tried.

- Aquarium salt (donated by a student with a saltwater fish tank who changed brands of salt)
- Baking soda (less noxious than salt, perhaps?)
- Borax (well, it's a strong glaze flux, maybe it'll do something)

- Copper sulphate
- Epsom salts (a source of magnesium, also a glaze flux)
- Ferric chloride (it does wonderful things in raku, though it's awfully noxious)
- Ice-Melt™ (another form of salt)
- Liquid iron plant food (maybe a safer source of iron color than the ferric chloride)
- Miracle-Gro™
- Pearl ash (a source of potassium, another glaze flux and very similar in action to sodium—maybe pearl ash will give similar results to salt)
- Trisodium phosphate (yet another source of sodium.)

With soluble chemicals, I've tried dissolving them in water and soaking wood shavings in the water, then drying them out and using them in my test pots. This is a lot of trouble and didn't seem to make any particular difference in the results, so I'm not bothering with that this time.

Often included in pit-firings, according to my research, are copper wire and steel wool, so one of my little test pots is wrapped in a chore boy copper scrubber and another in steel wool. I don't have any iron filings but in a later pit I'll try to get some to test. Other pots in this pit contain organic material with the shavings. I've often heard of people using banana peels (high in potassium) in pit firing, so I've looked for other high-potassium vegetable materials to try. The three I've thought of

are potato peels, avocado peels, and coffee grounds. The last organic I'm trying is used horse stall bedding. I simply filled one of the pots with this instead of the plain shavings. I happen to have access to large amounts of the stuff and, if it's good fertilizer, maybe it's good pot-food, too.

The Good, The Bad, and The Ugly

I've gotten pretty definitive results from some materials and disappointing results from others. Sometimes the pots end up in a relatively cool spot and come out with a lot of black on them, but then, it could be that if the black had burned off there would be spectacular colors underneath. I'll just have to try again to know for sure. I have found a couple of materials that may contribute some color, but they melt in the heat of the pit and form a crust on the pot. These are perhaps not such desirable materials to add to future firings.

The materials yielding positive results include all the salts as well as

These are some of the chemicals and other materials to be tested in isolation in the pit firing. In the back row are Miracle-Gro, ferric chloride, coppersulfate, liquid iron plant food, borax, Epsom salts, trisodium phosphate, salt, and baking soda. In the front are coffee grounds, a copper scrub pad, steel wool, banana peels and avocados.

Small pots are nestled into larger pots with various combinations of materials inside. Most contain a handful of wood shavings with a tablespoon of some chemical; some contain shavings with two chemicals; and some contain other materials such as banana peels and pieces of copper scrub pad.

the baking soda. All give yellow-orange color, with no particular difference between them that I can tell. Even Epsom salt leaves the same salt color. Trisodium phosphate left a pretty salt color, but it also fluxed inside its container and left a crusty deposit behind. Salt can have this effect, too, especially the coarser kinds of salt—a possible reason to use baking soda instead. Pearl ash fluxed in the pit, as well, but borax was the worst offender in this regard.

Banana peels left peach-colored marks; coffee grounds produced a vivid orange. Ferric chloride gave spectacular results though concerns about toxic fumes would make me hesitate to use it widely in a pit. I need to keep trying iron fertilizers, and get some iron filings. The test with the steel wool came out black, but I have seen steel wool leave rust-colored patches on pots. The copper scrubber produced black marks where it directly touched the pot, and green fuming near it. I was

surprised to find copper sulfate also producing lime green marks obviously the shavings burned away completely and the copper re-oxidized. Stall bedding gave promising results in one test, though another came out too black. I'll keep collecting it—at the very least it's a free source of shavings!

Practice Makes Perfect

My testing method is far from scientific, as it's hard to be sure that the contents of the bowls were really isolated from the atmosphere in the rest of the pit. Sometimes the success of a test is obvious, as with the banana-peel pot, which bears clear outlines of broken bits of dried banana peel. But over time I'll get better and better answers to my questions, as I try promising materials again and again in each firing. I am gradually building up an understanding of which chemicals and organics are worth putting into our pit.

Different clays are susceptible to being affected by different materials. Specifically, the B-mix clay I usually use will tend to pick up good reds from copper but little of the typical yellow salt color. When coated with a terra sigillata made from OM4 ball clay, the reverse is true.

Plans for the Future

One hypothesis I've formed is that while chemicals are the most reliable color producers—salt and copper sulfate remain the workhorses in our pit—it is possible that organics, while weaker in effect, are less

The silhouettes of pieces of dried banana peel are apparent around this pot, as well as a lovely soft ornage color.

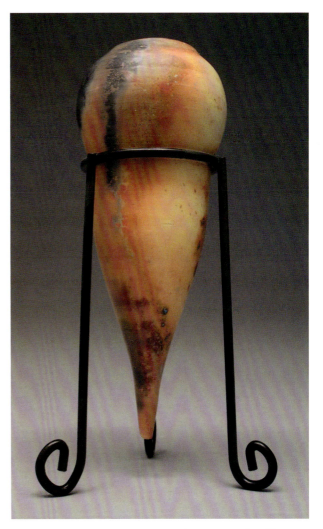

The bottom of this pot shows spectacular color from ferric chloride.

The orange color here seems to be typical of coffee grounds, although there is a little red toward the bottom of this piece so clearly it wasn't quite entirely isolated from the copper in the pit.

likely to flux and stick to the pots. It's like the difference between chemical and organic fertilizers in your garden. You need only a small amount of a chemical fertilizer, and if you use too much it will burn your plants. On the other hand, organic fertilizers have a weaker effect, but it's basically impossible to use too much. I just need to get a really good handle on which organic materials are actually effective in a pit, and how close they have to be to the pot to affect it.

So, into my next pit will go another batch of little test pots inside bowls. I hope to find ever more new materials to test, and get more definite answers about the pros and cons of the things I've already tried. Every time I will be a little better able to answer the "what will this material do" questions, and a little better able to direct the desired color towards a particular pot. In the meantime, I'm collecting an awful lot of little pots and bigger bowls of various colors!

Clockwise from upper left: Trisodium phosphate, ferric chloride, Miracle-Gro, and Epsom salts. All seem to yield similar yellow colors, although you can see a spot of red from the copper in the Miracle-Gro.

These three pots show the range of colors that various forms of copper can yield. The larger piece bears the typical red color deposited by fumes from copper sulphate. The small one on the upper left was buried in used horse stall bedding mixed with copper sulphate. The other small pot shows the black outline of a piece of copper scrub pad. This green color is typical in our pit near copper wire.

Pit Firing in North Carolina

by Dan and Linda Riggs

Ovoid vase, 8 inches in height, wheel-thrown stoneware, bisque fired to Cone 09, wrapped with steel wool and copper wire, gas fired to 1500°F in a loose saggar filled with oak chips, copper sulfate crystals, sea salt and seaweed, by Edge Barnes, Raleigh, North Carolina.

It was probably soon after the discovery of fire when early humans realized that heated clay became harder, more durable. The fact that clay could be imprinted with shapes and colors applied was an aesthetic plus. Today, the ancient technique of pit firing is becoming increasingly popular because of those aesthetic pleasures, although the shapes and surfaces of the pots reveal the modern touch of artistic form, as well as the calculated use of chemicals and just the right amount of sawdust and wood.

Edge Barnes and Zoie Holtzknecht, two potters from the Raleigh-Durham-Chapel Hill area of North Carolina, are among those who experiment with pit-firing techniques. Although they come from very different backgrounds, they share a passion for surface markings achieved by placing their bisque-fired pots, along with various chemicals and organic materials, in a sawdust- and wood-filled pit.

Barnes generally likes to burnish his leather-hard pots with a stone. This is followed by buffing with plastic or a soft cloth to increase the shine. Holtzknecht, on the other hand, likes a rougher finish and focuses more on developing color on the surfaces of her pots. Flashes of color on pit-fired ware are achieved by intimate contact with volatile materials, such as copper and salt.

For example, Barnes often wraps part of a Chore Boy copper scrub pad around a pot, holding the stretched wire in place with hot glue from a gun. The copper wire can also be covered with slabs of paper clay, which act like a saggar, trapping the vaporizing copper next to the surface.

A more conventional technique involves the addition of copper sulfate to a saggar. Barnes uses a metal bowl for the saggar, adds copper sulfate, then the copper-wire-wrapped pots, peanut shells, cotton balls and rock salt, covering the arrangement with an inverted ceramic bowl.

Copper mesh can be held in place with hot glue.

Metal and clay bowls are used as a saggar.

Thin slabs of paper clay will trap fumes near the surface.

Holtzknecht prepares a firing bundle with a mixture of volatiles and combustibles.

Another method involves placing the pot on a large piece of newspaper, wrapping or draping it with steel wool or copper wire, and sprinkling copper sulfate and rock salt over and around it. Combustibles, such as cotton balls, banana peels, dry dog food, dried flowers, etc., are then placed on the newspaper, which is subsequently rolled around the pot. The newspaper holds the sulfate, salt and combustibles in close proximity to the pot's surface, where they will add interesting designs and colors.

Once the pots are ready for the firing, the next step is to prepare the pit. For the firing shown here,

Barnes and Holtzknecht used a large pit, dug by a backhoe to a depth of about 16 inches. Some people prefer shallower pits to produce brighter colors; others prefer pits as deep as 4 feet.

Over a loose bed of wood and newspaper, they laid a course of very dry sawdust (4 to 5 inches thick). While the newspaper-wrapped pots and metal-bowl saggars could be nestled

Bowl, approximately
8 inches in diameter,
wheel-thrown stone-
ware, pit fired in oak
chips, surrounded by
copper sulfate, raw
cotton and coarse
steel wool, by
Zoie Holzknecht.

Bottle, 10 inches in
height, gas fired to
1500°F in a loose sag-
gar filled with oak
chips, copper sulfate,
sea salt, seaweed, steel
wool and copper wire,
by Edge Barnes.

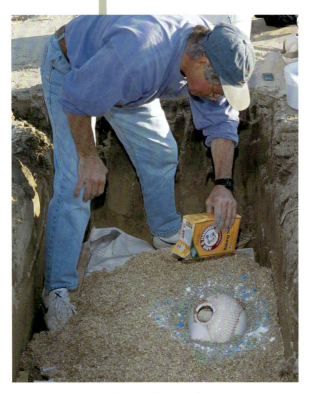

Edge Barnes sprinkling baking soda around a copper-wire-wrapped pot nestled in the sawdust.

Barnes carefully brushing aside ash and debris to remove the fired ware from the pit.

right next to one another in the sawdust, the "naked" pots were spaced several inches apart. Copper sulfate, baking soda and rock salt were then sprinkled around the pots. Dry dog or cat food, banana peels and seaweed could also be added.

A 2- to 3-inch-thick layer of sawdust was poured over the pots, then several feet of wood. Barnes prefers to use thin wood strips, as these burn much quicker and hotter than thicker pieces.

The fire was started with a torch in four or five places, so that the combustibles would burn evenly throughout the entire pit. When it had burned down somewhat, an-

other 1- to 2-foot layer of wood was added.

The pit was then left to burn out. The pots were retrieved only when they were cool enough to handle. Removing ware too early can cause cracking.

Pit-fired pots can be cleaned and lightly polished by rubbing with a cloth. For a brighter shine, wax can be applied; Barnes uses Butcher's Wax.

There are probably as many variations in pit-firing technique as there are potters, which makes every piece unique. The thrill of discovery exists each time the cooled ashes are pushed aside.

Black-Firing in a Barrel

by Sumi von Dassow

This burnished fluted pot illustrates the striking effect you can achieve by black-firing without a kiln.

Compared to pit-firing and raku, making pots simply black may sound like an easy task, but it can be surprisingly tricky. Certainly doing a raku-style post-firing reduction technique, without using glaze, makes pots black. But if you're doing burnished work with slip decoration in the manner of the Pueblo Indians, you may not want to risk damaging the surface by handling the pot with tongs.

Another approach to black-firing pots is to fire the pots buried in sawdust in a pit or in a brick box; however, for the sawdust to burn, there must be an air supply, and the result is that pots usually don't get completely black. In addition, there is also the potential problem with sawdust-firing burnished and decorated pottery of ash or soot sticking to the polished surface of the pot and ruining the burnish or obscuring the decoration.

To get around all these problems, I worked out a firing method that doesn't require lifting the pot with tongs, allows the firing to be completely smothered, and protects the pot from direct contact with the combustible materials being used. Indian potters fire their beautiful black pots by stacking them carefully on grates above the fire, surrounding and covering the stack with pot shards or sheets of metal, and smothering the fire once it's sufficiently hot by covering the entire mound with soil or ash. I wanted to find a way to achieve this same effect with less effort by firing inside a barrel.

The Partial Solution

I started by placing a layer of newspaper, sawdust, and wood scraps on the bottom of a trash can. On top of this, I added some bricks to elevate a barbecue grill over this pile of combustibles, then placed the pots on the grill. To protect the pots, each one was covered with a coffee can or popcorn tin into which I had punched holes to allow the smoke in. I then built a fire around and under the coffee cans with newspaper and kindling, adding larger pieces of wood as the fire took hold. Once the fire was burning merrily, I covered the trash can to create the same sort of smoke-filled environment present in a raku reduction barrel. Using this method, I was able to get my pots almost black—but I could see there was still some element lacking for perfect success.

Solving the Problem

The problem seemed to be that, inside a barrel, the fire just wasn't getting quite hot enough. I reasoned that the sides of the trash can blocked the fire from getting adequate air for maximum heat pro-

I use Navajo Wheel clay from Industrial Minerals Company for all my burnished and smoke-fired pottery. It is a cone 6 red clay that burnishes easily, and is very durable even when fired at such low temperatures.

duction, so the pots inside weren't very receptive to the smoke. I realized that to raise the temperature of the fire, I needed to get more air into the barrel, and the best way to do that would be to blow it in. I literally needed to fan the flames. The next time I tried barrel-firing, I held an electric fan over the barrel before covering it, and the result was a barrel full of beautiful shiny black pots!

This firing method has proved ideal for workshops, as well as for an individual potter firing alone, a few pots at a time. The only materials needed for the firing are a trash can, a grill or rack of some sort—even simply a piece of sturdy metal screen—one or more perforated cans, a fan, and fuel.

Before the smoke firing, I usually bisque-fire the pieces to cone 018—any higher and the burnish is lost, any lower and the pot isn't vitrified. I've tried smoke-firing greenware, and as long as the temperature isn't raised too quickly and enough wood is used to get the fire burning quite hot, the ware seemed to have reached approximately cone 018. (It rings when tapped, and doesn't disintegrate in water although a burnished pot will be damaged if left to sit full of water).

We loaded a barrel with newspaper, a bit of sawdust, wood scraps from a cabinet shop, and charcoal briquettes. The barbecue grill is supported on bricks above these materials (figure 1).

A burnished pot is placed onto the grill (figure 2). The pot has been bisqued to cone 018 and preheated in an electric kiln for an hour on low before placing it in the barrel.

The barrel is loaded with six pots inside coffee cans (figure 3). Note the holes in the coffee cans.

Scrap wood is loaded around the coffee cans (figure 4). One more pot has been loaded, beginning a second layer. Note: Pots in an upper layer often do not come out as black, and overfilling the barrel can reduce air circulation and prevent the barrel from getting hot enough.

Once the fire is lit, an electric fan is aimed into the barrel to increase the heat (figure 5). Be careful the cord doesn't touch the side of the hot barrel.

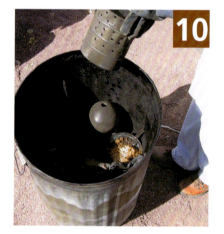

The fire is burning merrily (fig. 6).

Sawdust is dampened with a spray bottle and is the last ingredient to be added to the barrel (figure 7). Damp sawdust may promote the development of a silvery black surface, instead of a plain ebony black.

The damp sawdust is poured into the barrel to create smoke (figure 8). Although the flames aren't dramatic at this point, notice that the fire is burning well underneath the grill.

As soon as the sawdust is poured in, the lid is placed on the barrel to trap the smoke (figure 9). The barrel will smoke heavily for a few minutes after the lid is put on.

Once the outside of the barrel is cool enough to touch (about an hour) it can be opened (figure 10). Notice that the fuel hasn't all burned, but the pot is black.

Gabriele Koch
Primitive Perfection

by Tony Birks

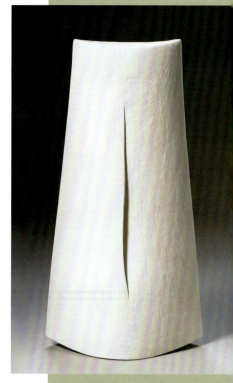

**"White Tower,"
17 inches in height,
handbuilt T-Material,
with slips, burnished
and smoke fired.**

The naturalist and filmmaker Sir David Attenborough is an enthusiastic collector. His collection is wide-ranging, with the emphasis more on artifact than on fine art. It includes things made for the improvement of the quality of life in primitive cultures as well as modern civilization.

To have this life-enhancing function, a tool or a pot can be useful and beautiful, and it is particularly the sculptural quality which Attenborough seeks out, and which defines his collection. Amongst modern potters whose work is included in the collection are Dame Lucie Rie, from whose long career are included items made more than 40 years apart, and Gabriele Koch, still in mid career, whose work he has admired and collected for many years. Indeed, he has written the introduction to the monograph on Koch's work, which first appeared ten years ago.

Apart from the fact that both Rie and Koch came to Britain to flower as artists from their native Austrian and German backgrounds, there is little in common between Rie the wheel thrower and Koch the hand-builder, except for the tremendously high standard that each sets for her work, a perfectionism which infuses everything. However, it is worth mentioning the high regard that Rie had for Koch's work. It was she who first drew the attention of the present writer to the pots of Koch nearly twenty years ago, when Koch was just making her name for burnished and smoke-fired ware.

There are some who say that the burnish/smoke-fire technique is limited, and that to restrict oneself to it to the exclusion of all else is to be confined. It does not seem so to me, or to Koch, who finds immense opportunities for experimentation and refinement within the self-imposed restrictions of this method. In her brief, but carefully considered personal statement she says, "I am interested in the vessel as an abstract sculptural object. I am concentrating on simple essential forms, which sometimes emphasize the relationship between internal and external space; of movement or stillness within the form."

Amphora, 19 inches in height, hand-built T-Material, with slips, burnished and smoke fired.

In a few words, she is describing ceramic sculpture at its best, where the undeniably attractive and compelling concept of the vessel is refined and developed to please the eye. The vessels she makes are in good company. They are at home alongside Attic vessels, pre-Columbian Pueblo pots, the more humble domestic ware of India or North Africa, and of course other fine modern ceramics.

Though many potters, both amateur and professional, practice both handbuilding and smoke firing, Koch is one of very few in Britain whose career is founded exclusively on this specialized combined technique. She is often bracketed with the Nigerian–born Magdalene Odundo for no better reason than that these two women are the leaders in this field in Britain, for their work is unalike. Odundo's work is African in inspiration and form, whereas Koch's work, originally inspired by peasant work seen in anthropological museums, or firsthand in Spain or Mexico, has moved away from domestic functional shapes to more refined forms on which mathematics and architecture have had more bearing. One might add music, with its mathematical intervals that relate to geometry and proportion, although the potter would find such an analogy pretentious. Indeed, Koch is very unpretentious about her work. Rie, largely to fend off searching questions about her motives when she had become world famous, would say, "I am just making pots." Underlying this, unsaid, is the essential "I am trying to make better pots."

And so it is with Koch. She explains, "I am not trying to make just any new form: this would be like inventing something for the sake of invention, trying to be clever. My interest lies in organic development, where one form contains the seed for the next one, where form is rooted in its own family tree."

She works alone in a clean white studio in north London, sometimes building several pots at once, or rather having various pots at various stages. Slow drying is an essential requirement for forms that are to be slipped and burnished, and each one has to be caught and carried forward at precisely the right time. Thus, in the interests of efficiency and production, perhaps four or five forms are in process at once. Interestingly, there is usually wide variety amongst these forms. She may be in the process of producing a series of very similar pots as one shape evolves from another, but, perhaps because of her order book, or because she wants ideas to bounce from one form to another, she can be working on a sphere, an open bowl, a rectilinear tower and an attenuated bullet form all at once.

Applying colored slip to the drying form is time consuming as several layers are needed, one wet layer over another layer that is drying, and her spectrum of slips is slowly changing. Her earliest work was in earth colors—brown, red/brown or ochre. She still uses these colors from time to

"Blue Tower," 12 inches in height, handbuilt T-Material, with slips, burnished and smoke fired. While T-Material offers incredible strength to Koch's handbuilt forms, extremely close attention must be paid to the drying process; the timing of slip application and burnishing are crucial.

time, but has introduced a vibrant blue, a beautiful duck-egg green and (my favorite) an orange color, which is organic, somewhere between a ripe apricot and a chestnut.

Taking perhaps 200 times as long to make a single pot than a repeat thrower means that her work, so labor intensive, is restricted in number. She works very hard, but makes few pots. She wants to be judged by the results; nothing that fails to match up to her standards is allowed to reach the marketplace.

Dimpled vessel, 12 inches in height, hand-built T-Material, with slips, burnished and smoke fired, by Gabriele Koch.

The Flexibility of Smoke Firing

After the slow first firing in a gas kiln to 1740°F is completed, Koch places the pot, vertically or at an angle, in a garbage bin kiln or any sort of metal container—sometimes an old oil drum.

For really large pots, she may build a special kiln from firebricks joined with sticky clay, but the kiln is just a container for the heat, and how it is made or of what is unimportant. What is important is how she packs the pots inside and out with a mixture of different kinds of sawdust. It is her choice of sawdust and the density of the packing—how hard she presses the sawdust against the pot's surface—that gives her control of the patterning, and she chooses this to suit each pot. The result does not always please her, in which case the patterning can be fired away in a standard gas kiln to a temperature of 1470°F and smoke fired again in a new batch of sawdust. So, like a stage performance, or another "take" on film, or a piece of bronze casting where the patination needs to be stripped off chemically and done again, she can work on her perfect form until it has a perfect marriage with its smoky, carbonized surface.

For traveling potters or collectors who want to see her work, there is ample opportunity in European museums and public collections. If you have not yet seen Koch's work to try hard to do so: it is a rewarding, special experience. A list of all public collections with her work is included in a monograph of her work, published by Marston House Publishers.

Koch occasionally, but rarely give lectures and demonstrations. It takes a lot to persuade her to do a demonstration tour far from London, as she has to take enough of her preferred molochite-rich clay and her slips. Also, she needs to have work half-made to show students or the demonstrations would take several days. In her lectures she pays homage to sources of her inspiration—Claudi Casanovas, Hans Coper, Peter Voulkos and Paul Soldner; but more significantly I think, the Catalan artist Antoni Tapies, and also the dry, hot Spanish landscapes that first drew her to work in the field of earth and fire.

Successful Barrel Firing

by Paul Wandless

The smells and sounds of a crackling campfire are among my fondest childhood memories. My father taught my brother Dan and me how to gather and split wood, and start and maintain campfires. This may explain why barrel firing is one of my favorite methods of finishing work. For many artists, the process and experience of outdoor firing is just as fun and exciting as the results achieved.

Barrel-fired work produces beautiful black and gray smoke patterns, and blushes of maroon, pink, earthy orange and yellow ochre from differ-ent chemical colorants introduced. Firing in a barrel is simple, but getting results you like can be elusive at times. Here are four basic tips I've developed over the years:

- Prepare the work properly to take maximum advantage of the heat, smoke and fumes
- Use the right combustibles and chemicals for colorants when packing the barrel
- Have enough hot embers to burn all the combustibles
- Leave work in the barrel the proper length of time

Another important factor is to have realistic expectations of the achievable results. Every firing process has certain parameters of what can be achieved. Many of the colors are subtle and it may take more than one firing to get the desired effects. And, while barrel firing creates strong contrasts between darks and lights with blushes and flashes of color, you won't get the cherry reds, true oranges and bright yellows of traditional glazes and slips. This isn't to say the colors aren't lush or rich, only that it's important to know what's achievable with this process. With enough experimenting and experience, a wide variety of vibrant colors can be achieved with contrast and intensity.

Green Stage

The clay body color and temperature to which you bisque fire determines whether or not you're going to get the most out of the conditions and atmosphere in the barrel. Porcelain, white or light-colored clay bodies work best to show the more subtle surface colors created from the smoke and chemical colorants. My clay body is more of a buff color, so I brush a thin coat of white slip (80% EPK kaolin and 20% Ferro Frit 3124) onto leather-hard work to ensure a light surface for the firing (figure 1). After bisque firing, I use white or light-colored Amaco Velvet Underglazes because of their fine particle size and the broad palette of colors. Use darker clay bodies and surfaces if you prefer deeper values

and richer blacks. Another option is to burnish your work while still green. You can apply terra sigillata before burnishing or simply polish the clay surface itself.

Bisque Stage

Since this is a low-temperature, atmospheric firing, a soft bisque (cone 010 to 06) is best to keep the clay body porous enough for smoke and fumes to penetrate the surface. This one step alone can dramatically change the results possible during firing. Bisque your clay body at a few different temperatures (for example, cones 010, 08, 06) and see which works best with your clay for the results you want. After bisque firing, there are still more decorative techniques to experiment with to create interesting effects. My favorite is to wrap copper wire around the work, which leaves deep maroon to black lines where it touches the surface (figure 2). The wire gets brittle and breaks off after the firing. Another option is to apply a salt wash or ferric chloride to the bisqued piece. A salt wash introduces sodium, which aids in developing some yellow and ochre blushes. Soak cheesecloth in a salt solution and wrap it around the piece or brush salt onto the bisque in select areas. Applying a 50/50 solution of water and ferric chloride produces light orange to rust colors. I use a siphon blower to apply ferric chloride (figure 3).

You can also barrel fire a piece of low-fire glazed work (figure 4) for some interesting results. Get a fake raku effect where smoke is forced into the cracks of a gloss or crackle glaze, or change the color of the glaze with fuming and direct contact with the colorants in the barrel. To get consistent results, do several tests and keep good notes on the glazes and chemicals you used.

Firing Tools

For a barrel, you can use a full-sized 55-gallon metal drum, a smaller metal can or even a drum cut in half. It all depends on the amount and size of work being fired. If using a full-sized drum, drill or punch ¼-inch diameter holes around the bottom, middle and top about a foot apart to increase the amount of oxygen and keep the embers burning (figure 5). Avoid chrome trashcans and thin-walled containers. The intense heat melts the chrome or paint off the sides, releasing pungent and sometimes dangerous fumes, and the thin walls get brittle over time.

Arrange all combustibles and colorants within easy reach (figure

For best effects, begin with a white body or brush white slip onto a tinted body.

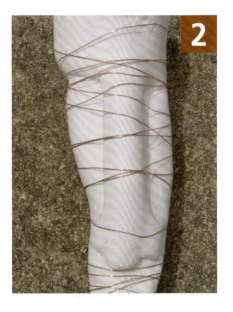

Piece with white slip and wrapped with copper wire.

WARNING

Be extremely careful not to inhale ferric chloride or allow any contact with lips. Wear rubber or latex gloves and apply it outdoors or in a spray booth. Ferric chloride is a corrosive chemical used as a copper etchant and should be handled with proper care.

The author carefully spraying ferric chloride on pot (see warning).

Covered jar with cone 05 crackle glaze fired over white slip. This jar is seen in figure 8.

Use a 55-gallon drum or a heavy, metal trash can with lid. Make ¼-inch holes 1 foot apart to aid combustion.

Combustible examples: straw, sawdust, newspaper, wood. (Do not use any pressure-treated materials).

Various colorants (L-R) red iron oxide, Miracle Gro, copper carbonate, salt.

6). For colorants, use red iron oxide, copper carbonate, Miracle-Gro (copper sulphate) and/or coarse salt (figure 7). Combustibles include wood (kindling, branches, scrap wood) sawdust, straw and newspaper. Warning: Do not burn any pressure-treated lumber or sawdust. Fumes are toxic.

Packing

There are several ways to approach barrel firing and each has interesting results. You can use more sawdust for heavier smoke or more straw for a faster firing with less smoke—I'm somewhere in the middle. Use the following recommended approach, then experiment with different combinations of materials. You'll find each firing varies depending on the work, combustibles, colorants, weather conditions, heat achieved and length of firing. Trial and error is the best teacher, so keep good notes on the variables for each firing.

Start with an empty container and make a 2- or 3-inch sawdust bed in the bottom mixed with a little straw. Next, generously sprinkle colorants on top of the sawdust bed then place your work on top (figure 8). Colorants beneath the work help to develop color on the underside from the direct contact, and will also fume up the sides.

Pack the barrel in layers keeping in mind that as embers burn, your pieces may fall and shift. Be sure to space out the work a little to avoid unwanted contact from the shifting during firing. After all work is in place, put more sawdust, straw, and small twigs or kindling in and around the work (figure 9). Don't pack the combustible materials too densely. It's good to have air pockets to help keep the embers burning. A tightly packed barrel burns slower, smokes heavier and may choke out after a few hours and need to be re-lit. A looser pack burns a little faster and achieves a wider variety of colors. I like the faster burning barrel and the more subtle effects mixed with heavy smoke at the end from the smoldering sawdust bed.

After completely covering the work with combustibles, sprinkle more colorants on top (figure 10). This gives the embers another layer of colorants to burn, and heat to create fumes that affect the tops of the works and fall down the sides as well. Add another inch of sawdust to complete the layering (figure 11).

This completes one level of packing and I normally fire only this amount. Sometimes, if I have alot of work, I repeat the layering process and make another level of combustibles and colorants. I can usually make three levels in a 55-gallon drum, and stop layering combustibles about a foot below the rim of the container, filling that space with crumpled newspaper and small and large pieces of wood (figure 12).

Firing

Light the newspaper and let it burn away (figure 13). For safety, the fire must be contained inside the can, so don't stack any wood above the

SOURCES OF COLOR	
Copper carbonate, copper wire, Miracle Gro (Contains copper sulp]hate)	Flashings of deep red to maroon and shades of pink
Salt or salt wash, baking soda and seaweed	Introduces sodium and gives flashes of yellow and ochre
Red iron oxide and ferric chloride	Flashes of earthtones from peach to rust

rim. As the wood burns, continue to add more so the fire stays strong for about 20 to 30 minutes. This ensures reaching maximum heat and creating a good bed of embers to burn through all the combustibles. It will take about an hour for the fire to burn down to a bed of white-hot embers that will smolder and make their way to the bottom. Use a metal rod to prod the embers to be sure the fire below the surface hasn't stalled out (figure 14) since it is not uncommon to have to relight the fire if it goes out.

It takes about 5–7 hours to burn to the bottom of a barrel with one level of combustible. By the end of the firing, only ashes and work should remain—a sign of a good firing. Don't be surprised if some of the work cracked or broke from thermal shock. This is common with all alternative firing processes due to the quickness of heating and cooling.

If you have to leave the barrel unattended, it must be covered so sparks don't fly. Even if the flames have died down, a strong breeze could breathe new life into the fire.

Sawdust bed with colorants added and work in place.

Sawdust added along with more colorants and other combustibles.

First layer of combustibles added includes straw and wood.

Add a final layer of combustibles including an inch of sawdust.

Set a fire with crumpled newspapers and dry wood.

Allow the fire to burn and keep it stoked for 20–30 minutes.

Carefully agitate embers with a metal rod to loosen packed materials and encourage complete combustion.

If you need to leave the can during the firing, secure a lid to prevent sparks from escaping.

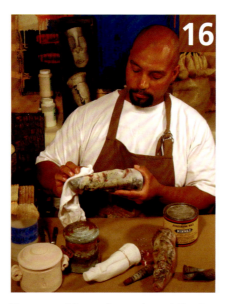

You can add a patina to barrel-fired work by cleaning and polishing the pieces with wax. For supplies, you'll need latex gloves, paste wax, sponge, nylon brush and a soft cloth.

Four barrel-fired heads: (L-R), head sprayed with ferric chloride; head with white slip and copper wire; head with white underglaze and copper wire; head with deep yellow underglaze and ferric chloride. All heads were polished with paste wax.

I use softbrick as spacers and as a weight for the lid (figure 15). This setup allows air to get in the barrel so you don't smother the embers and is the same setup used to smolder the barrel overnight.

Finishing and Cleaning up

When the barrel has cooled, remove the work and wash it off with water and a soft cloth. For hard-to-remove ash and residue, use a soft nylon brush. Stay away from abrasive or metal brushes that could scrape the work. If you end up with a piece that didn't take the smoke and color well, fire it again in the next barrel. For safety, always douse the container with water to assure all embers are extinguished.

The surface is typically a dry, matt finish if the work wasn't burnished, but it can be polished. Paste wax will deepen many of the subtle colors. Apply a thin coat and let dry 3–5 minutes before polishing with a soft cloth (figure 16). I also use the soft nylon brush to polish the surface and get the wax out of any crevices.

There's no one way to barrel fire and get perfect results, but these barrel basics will ensure a level of success each firing. Experiment with other combustible materials and colorants and see the variety of finishes that can be achieved. Good luck and enjoy the fire.

Saggar Firing with Aluminum Foil

by Paul Wandless

Saggar firing is an alternative firing process with several variations on how the technique can be used. The word "saggar" is thought to have come from the word "safeguard" due to its use as a protective casing. Traditional saggars were reusable refractory containers that would protect ceramic ware from the smoke, fumes or flying ash of wood or coal kilns. The opposite is true today since we want all the carbon and fumes inside the container!

Think of a saggar as a container that creates and holds a mini-atmosphere surrounding your piece. This atmosphere is comprised of burning combustible materials that fume and smoke the clay surface during the firing process. One common kind of saggar is a clay or metal container that allows for about 4–6 inches of space around your clay work. The space around the clay work is filled with all the combustible organic materials, oxides, salt, soda ash and other chemicals that you want to create your colors. The atmosphere of smoke and fumes stay inside the saggar and carbonize, flash and blush the surface of your piece. This type of saggar can be fired in a gas, electric or raku kiln. Depending on what you put in the saggar to make color, this kind of saggar firing works at any temperature, so you can go to cone 10 if you like and get good results. Some saggar containers (especially those used between cone 01 or cone 10) have small holes in the walls to help it vent a little and also

to prevent pressure from building up inside and blowing the lid off.

Aluminum Foil Saggars

Aluminum foil saggar firing is a different approach that's meant to work exclusively at lower temperatures. You can get results as low as 1500ºF up to around 1850ºF. The firing is performed in a pit, barrel or raku kiln and relies mostly on local reduction and the fuming of chemicals to get visual results. In place of a metal or clay container, heavy-duty aluminum foil is used to create the saggar that surrounds the clay work. Wrapped around the piece, heavy-duty aluminum foil holds all the combustible materials in place against the surface to fume and

flash. I like to think of this process as the "baked potato" approach to firing. Just like all the seasonings are held in place by the foil to soak into a potato when you bake it, all your combustibles are held in place to "season" your clay.

What to Expect

As with any alternative firing process, getting successful results on the first try can be elusive and unpredictable. Preparing your pieces properly to take full advantage of the fuming materials in the saggar atmosphere is the best way to achieve good results. Another important factor for alternative firing is having realistic expectations of achievable results. Every firing technique has certain parameters for what can be achieved visually on the surface. Many of the colors are subtle and it often takes more than one firing to achieve the visual effects you want.

Preparing Your Work

For this saggar firing technique, you'll need bisqueware, brushes and underglazes, and a clear low-fire liner glaze (figure 1). The color of the clay and the temperature you bisque fire at strongly influence surface effects. Porcelain, white or light-colored clay bodies allow the creation of more subtle colors on the surface, while a soft bisque (cone 010–06) keeps the clay body porous enough for fumes to better penetrate the surface. Bisque your clay body at different temperatures (e.g., cone 010, 08, 06) to see which porosity works best. If you prefer deeper values and richer blacks, use darker clay bodies and surfaces. Another option is to burnish your work while still green to give it a smooth satin surface after it's bisque fired. You can apply terra sigillata before burnishing or simply polish the clay surface itself.

In these examples, all work was made using a cone 7, buff stoneware bisque-fired to cone 04. If you don't use a white clay body, brush a thin coat of white slip on the bisque to assure a light surface (figure 2).

For variety, use commercial white and other light-colored underglazes (I use Amaco Velvet Underglazes) on the surface and mask off areas with painters tape to make designs (figure 3). Even simple stripes add variety and make all the difference

Sources of Color

Foil saggars produce strong contrasts between darks and lights, with blushes and flashes of color from a palette of earth-tone hues. The temperature reached inside the kiln and length of firing also greatly affect the color results. The strongest colors appear from local reduction, which is where direct contact is made between the surface and the materials. Here are a few examples of materials to use but not a complete list. Experiment with other oxides, carbonates and combustible materials that fume to see what else you can create on the surfaces of your work. The temperature the kiln reaches and how long you fire also affect your results. Keep good notes of every firing.

- Oxides, salt and soda ash washes yield fairly strong colors depending on the strength of the mixed solution. Fuming in the gaps between the surface and foil creates more subtle flashes of colors.
- Copper carbonate gives flashings of deep red to maroon and shades of pink.
- Copper wire can result in the same colors but, when in contact with the surface, often just leaves behind black lines.
- Miracle-Gro®, which contains copper sulphate, also produces the same hues and colors as copper carbonate, but it's a stronger chemical to work with. If it comes in direct contact with the surface or too much is used, it can leave a crusty, dark green or black surface.
- Salt/salt washes, baking soda, soda ash/soda ash washes and seaweeds introduce sodium and give flashes of pale yellow and ochre. Sodium washes work very well when brushed or sprayed on the surface. Wrapping cheese cloth soaked in the washes around the pot also results in stronger effects.
- Red iron oxide gives flashes of earth tones from peach to rust
- Liquid ferric chloride will give a range of earth tone colors that includes rusty oranges, browns, and even brick reds if used at full strength. These colors can be very overpowering due to the strength of this chemical and visually overwhelm all of your other materials in the saggar. When diluted 50/50 with water the hues are lighter and lean toward peach and tan.

CAUTION

Copper sulphate is a very powerful chemical and should only be handled while wearing protective latex or rubber gloves. Ferric chloride is a very powerful copper etchant and should only be handled while wearing protective gloves and a respirator for vapors.

on a finished piece. Sometimes I just use the colored underglazes to paint the rims and get some drips down the body (figures 4 and 5). I use a cone 04 white glaze on the inside of all the pots and drip the white glaze on the outside of them as well. Once all underglaze and glaze is applied, refire the work to cone 04 (figure 6).

Preparation

Gather the materials you'll need for your saggar (figure 7). The aluminum foil must be heavy duty. For this firing, I used course and fine sea salt, red iron oxide, liquid ferric chloride and Miracle-Gro. I do everything outdoors next to the kiln and immediately load and fire as soon as the saggars are done.

Choose a pot and tear off three lengths of aluminum foil. Each sheet of foil should be long enough to wrap completely around the pot. Crinkle up all of the foil and lay them down on your work surface (figure 8). The crinkled foil creates pockets that trap the materials and fumes against the surface for fuming.

I like to wrap copper wire around the work, which leaves deep maroon to black lines where it touches the surface (figure 9). Other options at this point include applying salt or soda washes or the liquid ferric chloride to the surface of the bisqueware.

After applying wire and washes, lay down the sheets of crinkled-up

aluminum foil in a criss-cross pattern on your work surface and place your pot in the middle. Start sprinkling each dry combustible material, one at a time, on the pot, using about 2 tablespoons of each material (figure 10). I do this by sight and am usually fairly liberal with the colorants to assure some kind of color results. Experiment with your own proportions for a few firings to get the exact kind of flashings of color you want.

After adding all the ingredients, slowly fold the foil up and around the pot (figure 11) being careful not to spill any of the materials, and gently press the foil against the surface (figure 12). You want it to touch the surface, but not have it pressing flat against it. The crinkled foil needs to have pockets of space around the form so the materials and fumes can be kept in place. The foil also leaves a light pattern where it touches the surface, but if the foil is pressed too tightly against the surface, colors won't develop. You can wrap additional sheets around the piece if you think you need more to keep it together. Remember that the longer the foil stays intact, the longer the work fumes. As soon as the foil starts to disintegrate at the end of the firing and holes are formed in the saggar, the fumes will escape. This is why heavy-duty foil is used because it takes longer to burn away.

Pick up the foil saggar and roll it around in the air so all the materials can tumble evenly around the piece. It should sound like a rattle. If you can't hear any noise, your foil is pressed too tightly against the surface. Now place the piece in the raku kiln (figure 13). You can tumble stack the work or just place them all next to each other depending on how many you're firing.

Firing

Firing foil saggars is pretty straight-forward, but just be sure to load them so you can clearly see them through an opening in your kiln. The firing should take about 45–60 minutes and reach a temperature of 1500–1800°F. I reach about 1000°F in about 30 minutes, at which point the kiln will show a little color and the foil starts to sag and looks a little thin. Then I let it continue to climb the last 500–800°F over the next 15–30 minutes. Once the foil starts to burn away, the saggar no longer holds in the fumes so the firing is complete. When you look inside, there will be a strong orange color, maybe some green or blue in the flames from the copper burning and the foil disintegrating. If you let it go a little longer, you'll lose a lot of the subtle colors. The optimal experience is for the aluminum foil to start burning away when you hit 1500–1700°F, but you may find that you can get satisfactory results as low as 1400°F. Let the kiln cool slowly before removing work to prevent cooling cracks. On your first firing, stop when the foil saggar first starts to break down. I fire by simply looking into the kiln, but you can use a hand-held pyrometer to be more accurate about your temperatures and to avoid overfiring.

I normally let a lot of the foil burn away and am left with mostly the stronger saggar effects (figure 14). Since I use a lot of colored slips on my work, this works for me visually. The amount of work you fire, proportions and types of combustibles, size of the kiln and size of your burner all factor into your timing and what effects you'll get. After one or two firings, you'll have a good sense of how to fire your work to get the results you want. Experiment with your own firing schedules to see what you like best. Keep good notes so you can duplicate the successful preparations and firings. Pieces you're unhappy with can always be rewrapped and refired.

Cleaning and Sealing

After about an hour, the work should be cooled and ready to be removed and cleaned. Use water, a rag and a stiff nylon brush to scrub off the foil and other residue from the surface of the pot (figure 15). Avoid abrasive or metal brushes that could scrape the surface. Once scrubbed, dunk the piece in a bucket of water and lightly scrub a little more just to make sure it's clean (figure 16). The wet surface is always beautiful and rich and this is when I decide which ones are keepers and which ones need to be re-wrapped and re-fired.

After drying, the surface will typically have a dry matt look, especially if the work wasn't burnished. To achieve the look it had when wet, using paste wax on the surface will deepen many of the subtle colors and bring back the richness. It also gives the surface a light sheen, but won't get glossy. Apply a thin coat of paste wax with a rag, let dry 3–5 minutes, then polish with a soft cloth. Use a soft nylon brush to polish the surface and get the wax out of any crevices.

Final Thoughts

As with all alternative firing processes, there's no one specific way to foil saggar fire and get perfect results. Talk to five different people and you'll get five different approaches to firing saggars. Practice and experience ultimately determines the best approach for your work. Experiment with other combustible materials and colorants in different combinations and proportions and you'll see the variety of finishes that can be achieved. In addition, stop firing at different temperatures and see how that affects your surfaces. Most importantly though, keep good notes on every detail at every step so you can duplicate successful results.

Martha Puckett
Porta-Kiln Barrel Firing

by Ginny Marsh

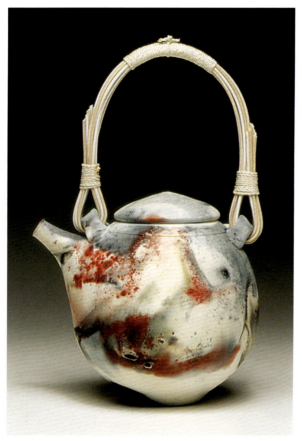

Teapot, 9 inches in height. All functional pieces are glazed on the interior with a matt transparent glaze and fired to cone 05 prior to the final sawdust firing in the porta-kiln.

Except for a few pots in the yard, the outside of Martha Puckett's house looks like the others in this older neighborhood on a tree-lined street in Louisville, Kentucky. Even the living room might fool you, and you might think she collects pots or even knows some potters. But if you get as far as the sun-room and see the dusty foot-

prints, you know the neighbors just wouldn't understand.

In the middle of the sun-room sits a potter's wheel surrounded by boxes of clay. Nearby is a wedging board and shelves. All of it is overlaid with the clutter of partially finished porcelain pots, tools, notes and posters. In the large project room at the back of the house, she periodically makes reed handles for some of her work. To keep fumes out of the house, the electric kiln is in the garage.

As a graduate student in the 1980s, Martha attended a workshop presented by John Leach, and from seeing his individual work, became interested in the effects of smoke on pots fired in saggars filled with sawdust. After trying this technique, she soon started experimenting with other firing techniques that allow the smoke to mark the clay body. It was sawdust firing that really excited her, with surfaces as smooth as the wings of a butterfly, and the dark and light swirling patterns of smoke and fire left on the work. Soon, she learned to introduce colors to her work and found this gave her pots that seemed like a private universe.

The Pots

More intuitive than technical in approach, and with limited space and resources, Martha learned to restrict her materials to those that were inexpensive and easy to acquire. Having found that a smooth white body best displays the luminous effects of the fire, she throws her work from a mixture of porcelain and white stoneware. The addition of the white stoneware makes a stronger pot, less prone to cracking from the shock of the sawdust firing. Martha uses 3 parts Standard Ceramic's Porcelain Body 130 to 1 part Standard White Stoneware 182.

Finding that simple forms with wide smooth surface areas best display the effects of sawdust firing, she smooths off any unwanted marks with a used nylon stocking rolled up and stuffed into its toe to make a soft lump easily held in the hand.

After bisque firing the work to cone 05, she applies a matt transparent glaze on the inside of utilitarian pieces, such as cups or teapots, and forms with rims that have been designed to be glazed. Glazed pieces are then bisque fired to cone 05 in an electric kiln prior to sawdust firing. The glaze develops a crackle pattern in the smoking process.

The Kiln

Martha usually prepares the work and materials ahead and does the firing in the evening. She uses the following materials:

- One or more prepared pots (bisqued and glaze fired).
- A 3- to 5-gallon popcorn can with lid. Martha prepares the can by punching or cutting about 30 holes into the can. The holes are from pencil diameter to nickel-sized, and they're made with a large nail and a "church key." Holes are located on the bottom and around the lower portion of the can to allow air intake so the combustible contents of the can will burn.
- Two or three bricks, any kind. The bricks are placed under the can to promote air circulation and to keep the hot can off the ground.
- Coarse, dry sawdust. Wood shavings leave too many air spaces and burn too quickly for adequate reduction and temperature gain, while very fine sawdust packs down, and leaves inadequate air spaces for sustained combustion.
- Wood chips. Martha gets small kiln-dried scraps from a local cabinet factory.
- A mixture of equal parts table salt and copper sulfate, perhaps 4 to 6 tablespoons per firing, if desired. Martha buys the impure copper sulfate sold in garden stores (used for controlling roots in drain pipes) instead of ceramic-grade copper sulfate. Table salt increases the tendency of the copper to volatilize.
- Lighter fluid and lighter stick or torch.
- Fireplace poker or a $^3/_8$- to $^1/_2$-inch diameter steel rod about 2 feet long.

The Firing

Martha has a half-dozen cans of slightly different sizes and with different configurations of holes in them; she fires one to six pots in each porta-kiln, and occasionally starts and tends up to three cans in one session. Her sawdust-firing process takes about two hours of active work and an additional three hours to allow the kiln to cool once the lid is placed on the can. She usually leaves her kiln to cool overnight.

Choose a safe and adequate space on a ground surface that will not burn. Martha likes to fire on an evening when there is no threat of inclement weather or wind.

Set the kiln on two or three bricks so the air can circulate under the kiln, and allow room to light the sawdust.

Fill the bottom of the can with 1 to 2 inches of coarse sawdust, pack the pots in the kiln, allowing at least an inch between them. Martha often places them upside down for the firing.

Sprinkle the mixture of copper sulfate and salt on the work (firgure 1). Note that the bowl is placed upside down and is resting on coarse sawdust.

Carefully cover the upper most pot(s) with at least 2 inches of woodchips and coarse sawdust above the top of the largest pot (figure 2). Fill the rest of the can with more sawdust.

After coating the top of the sawdust with charcoal lighter fluid, use a torch (like the kind used for charcoal grills) and light the fire (figure 3). CAUTION: Stand back and do not wear loose or synthetic clothing.

The porta-kiln should burn for an hour, more or less, according to the atmosphere, stirring the wood and adding more sawdust if necessary, until the pot can be seen glowing and the wood is burning well (figure 4). This is more easily seen in the low light of evening than in midday sunshine. Martha lets the sawdust smoke heavily at stages, and at other times removes the lid to encourage a fierce flame throughout the firing (figure 5). Smoke from reduction forces black carbon deep into clay while hot spots develop where the wood burns away, leaving white patches. The fire in cans with the larger holes burns more quickly and intensely, leaving relatively larger white areas on the pots than on the pots fired in cans with smaller holes. In the smoky reduction firing, copper typically turns red, but occa-

sionally a flare in the firing leaves bright green traces. Combined with salt, copper sulfate is highly volatile and fumes at the low temperature of 1470°–1650°F, giving varied and unexpected color effects.

When the work can be seen glowing, place the lid on top leaving a 1-inch opening. The placement will have to be watched for a few minutes and adjusted so that smoke continues to come out the open area. The firing is essentially finished about an hour after the lid is put on the porta-kiln.

The Results

By the next morning, in the brief quiet before work, Martha can remove the newly finished work from the cooled porta-kiln. The kiln often yields satisfying pots with a glimpse of a private world, but if she doesn't

Teapot and cups. Teapot is 10 inches in height (including handle) and the cups are 2½ inches in height.

like the results, she knows she can refire a piece up to 3 or 4 times without losing body strength.

Martha is always working on new variations on the shapes and firing technique. As you go out the door to the firing area in her small back yard, you may notice the small frame on the wall displaying an illustrated quote from William Blake's Auguries of Innocence:

To see a World
in a grain of sand,
And a Heaven
in a wildflower;
Hold infinity
in the palm of your hand,
And eternity in an hour.

Vessel, 4¾ inches in height, bisque fired to cone 05 in an electric kiln, then sawdust fired in the porta-kiln, using copper sulfate and salt in a reduction atmosphere.

Vessel, 6½ inches in height. Martha Puckett restricts herself to small precise pots, usually less than 8 inches tall.